Scrap Crafts Year 'Round

Scrap Crafts Year 'Round

More Than 70 Projects to Make with Less Than a Yard of Fabric

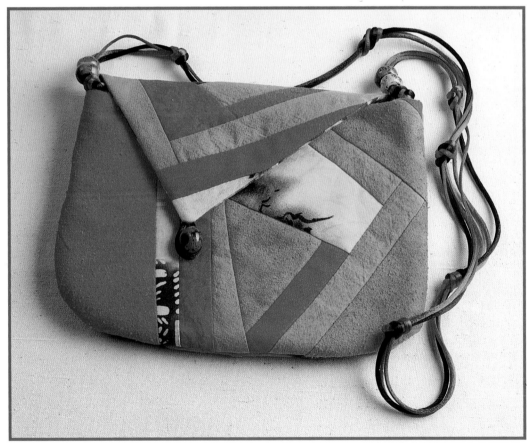

Chris Rankin

Sterling Publishing Co., Inc. New York
A Sterling/Lark Book

Editor: Carol Parks
Art Direction: Dana Irwin, Elaine Thompson
Photography: Evan Bracken, Light Reflections
Production: Elaine Thompson
Illustrations: Kay Holmes Stafford
Editorial assistance: Laura Dover, Valerie Anderson

Library of Congress Cataloging-in-Publication Data
Rankin, Chris.
    Scrap crafts year round : more than 70 projects to make
with less than a yard of fabric / Chris Rankin.
        p.   cm.
    "A Sterling/Lark book."
    Includes index.
    ISBN 0-8069-8166-0
    1. Textile crafts.   2. Gifts.   3. House furnishings.   4. Dress
accessories.   I. Title.
TT699.R35   1996
746--dc20   96-6015
                                                                 CIP

10 9 8 7 6 5 4 3 2 1

A Sterling/Lark Book

First paperback edition published in 1998 by
  Sterling Publishing Company, Inc.
  387 Park Avenue South, New York, N.Y. 10016

Produced by Altamont Press, Inc.
  50 College Street, Asheville, NC 28801

Distributed in Canada by Sterling Publishing
  % Canadian Manda Group, One Atlantic Avenue, Suite 105
  Toronto, Ontario, Canada M6K 3E7

Distributed in Great Britain and Europe by Cassell PLC
  Wellington House, 125 Strand, London WC2R 0BB, England

Distributed in Australia by Capricorn Link (Australia) Pty Ltd.
  P.O. Box 6651, Baulkham Hills, Business Centre, NSW 2153, Australia

Every effort has been made to ensure that all the information in this book is accurate.
However, due to differing conditions, tools, and individual skills, the publisher cannot be
responsible for any injuries, losses, and other damages which may result from the use of
the information in this book.

Printed in Hong Kong
Sterling ISBN 0-8069-8166-0 Trade
                  0-8069-8167-9 Paper

Contents

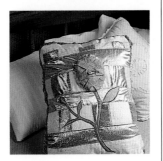

Introduction

Throughout a sewing lifetime, the typically ardent sewer accumulates enough scraps of fabric to tent Lake Superior, lengths of ribbons and trims that would reach from Galveston to Glasgow, and a stash of buttons that could fill a supertanker. Add to that a 6-inch square of each fusible interfacing on the market, a mile or two of elastic remnants (with no single piece long enough to encircle the waist), and 643 partial spools of thread in every known color except black or white. All of this must be carefully saved against times of shortage, or holocaust.

Many of the fabric bits of course have historical importance above and beyond their worth as mere cloth: pieces from your daughter's first prom dress, your own wedding dress, or perhaps the first garment you ever made. You must consider carefully before actually using them. But if you have been hoarding fabric for thirty years and have yet to begin your first quilt, or if you have already quilted for every significant person in your life, perhaps it's time to get that beautiful cloth out of storage and put it to use where it can be admired and appreciated.

The projects on these pages offer dozens of ideas for using your material wealth imaginatively. There are plenty of suggestions for dealing with those gift-giving occasions throughout the year that call for something unique and special—usually on short notice. There are lots of ways to quickly perk up a room before the visit of a Very Important Relative. And there are all kinds of accessories to add a fresh touch or distinctive note to the wardrobe.

Small Adornments

Infinitesimal scraps of fabric, pieces too small even to save for a quilt but too interesting to throw away, can be transformed into eye-catching jewelry and accessories. These little projects are a way to show off other tiny treasures too—bits of yarn, a single superb bead or button, even scraps of pretty paper and materials from nature. Craft and bead stores stock findings such as clasps for necklaces and bracelets, backs for pins and earrings, and barrettes to decorate.

A Pin in Two Parts

A fabric-covered triangle and semicircle are joined by beaded "fagoting" to make a most unusual pin. It's a great way to use up the smallest scraps, and a perfect setting to display a special button or bead. It's fun to try other combinations of shapes and materials, too.

For each shape, two pieces of cardboard are covered on one side with fabric, then glued together. Adding the decorative touches can take as little time as you have, or as much as you wish to spend. The finished pin is 2⅞ inches (7.3 cm) wide and 4¼ inches (10.8 cm) long, exclusive of the tassel.

DESIGNED BY LORI KERR

Materials

- Fabric for front and back
- Heavy non-corrugated cardboard
- Thin batting or fleece for padding
- Decorative cord, approximately ½ yard (.5 m)
- Approximately 6 dozen small bugle beads

- Buttons, lace, beads, or any other small ornaments to decorate the piece
- Tacky glue and, if desired, hot glue
- Paper-backed fusible web
- Strong polyester thread to match fabric
- Bar pin

Instructions

❶ Trace or photocopy the pattern. For fabric and fusible backing, cut a paper pattern for each design shape following the outer solid lines on the pattern pieces. For the cardboard and batting, cut to the inner dotted lines.

❷ Glue batting to a piece of cardboard large enough to accommodate both design shapes. Trace the designs on the back of the cardboard and cut them out.

❸ Cut two more design shapes from cardboard without batting.

❹ Cut two pieces of fusible web for each design shape. Fuse one of each to the fabric that will be used for the front of the pin, and the others to the back fabric. Cut out the shapes. Fuse the "front" fabric to the padded cardboard pieces, the other to the plain cardboard.

❺ Clip the fabric to the cardboard as necessary to fold under the edges smoothly. Fuse.

❻ Glue the back pieces to the fronts. Place under a weight and allow to dry.

❼ Glue cord around the edge of each piece.

❽ Position the pieces with an even distance between them and mark positions for sewing beaded strands that will connect the two.

❾ Thread a hand sewing needle that is fine enough to go through the beads. Use strong thread. Take several stitches just below the cord at one end of the lower piece. String beads as needed so that the strand is the correct length to bridge the distance. Take several stitches just below the cord on the upper piece. Take one or two short stitches, bringing the needle out at the next marked position. String beads again, using the same number as for the first strand, and take securing stitches in the lower piece. Continue along this way, and knot the thread securely when all the connectors are in place.

❿ Stitch or glue on any other embellishments, beaded tassels, or appropriate decorations. Attach the bar pin on the back of the upper piece with hot glue, or stitch it securely.

A Pin in Two Parts

Seam allowance included
Pattern shown actual size

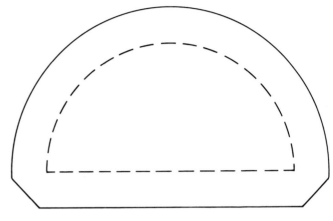

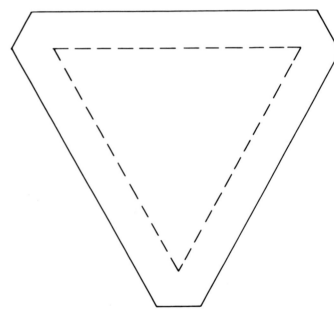

A Handful of Headbands

Headbands are always useful, quick to make, and take kindly to almost any sort of ornamentation you care to add. The red band in the photo is simplicity itself—a few lines of stitching with metallic thread on the outer side, and a bright cotton print on the reverse. The other band is pieced from silk and cotton fabrics, both solid colors and patterns, with one of the patterned fabrics used for the lining.

DESIGNED BY PAT TAYLOR

Materials

- Fabric for outer band, cut to pattern dimensions, or muslin this size and scraps for piecing

- Fabric for lining, the same as outer band

- ¾-inch (2-cm) elastic, 6½-inch (16.5 cm) length

Instructions

The band is a medium adult size. Check the fit before cutting the elastic and lengthen or shorten it if necessary.

❶ Enlarge the pattern and cut one outer band and one lining on the fold as indicated. If the band will be pieced, cut one muslin section by the pattern.

For the one-piece band:

❷ Work embellishment on the outer band section before construction. If the embroidery involves very dense stitching, use a tear-away or water-soluble backing.

For the pieced band:

Piece fabrics for the outer band onto the muslin, following the instructions on page 73.

❸ With right sides together, stitch outer fabric to lining along only the long edges with ¼ inch (.7 cm) seam allowance. Turn and press.

❹ Place one end of the elastic over one end of the outer band, overlapping by ½ inch (1.7 cm). Fold a small tuck in the band end to make it the same width as the elastic. On the right side, stitch the elastic to the band with a moderately wide zigzag stitch set at a very short stitch length. Stitch so the end of the elastic is encased in the stitching. Turn the band to the wrong side and stitch the band end to the elastic in the same way. Repeat for the other ends.

Tip: If your fabric permits, attach the elastic with a ballpoint needle to avoid piercing and weakening it.

Pattern is 50% of actual size.

PLACE ON FOLD

11

Essentials-Only Purses

DESIGNED BY JUDY ANDERSON

When your everyday handbag is too cumbersome or might spoil the effect of a fabulous outfit, put together a tiny envelope purse just large enough for lipstick, driver's license, and money to get you where you're going. The same pattern was used for both bags, but different fabrics and embellishments make each one unique. These bags are approximately 3½ inches (9 cm) square. It is a simple matter to enlarge the design if your own essentials occupy more space.

The white bag is made of soft, lightweight wool and lined with matching silk. The teal bag is silk inside and out, with the lining print also used for the strap and the flap appliqué.

12

DESIGNED BY JUDY ANDERSON

Materials

- Fabric for outer bag, one piece 4 inches (10 cm) wide and 11 inches (28 cm) long

- Fabric for lining, cut the same size

- Lightweight fusible interfacing for the flap if needed

- Decorative cord for strap, approximately 38 inches (1 m), or strip of fabric and cording to make a narrow fabric-covered cord

- Embellishments: beads (for the teal purse) or embroidery floss and a shisha mirror (white purse)

Instructions

Both purses are constructed in the same way.

❶ For very lightweight fabric, baste or sew interfacing to the wrong side of the flap.

❷ Add embellishment to the purse flap section.

For the white purse: The flap is trimmed diagonally, as shown on the diagram on the next page. French knots, double cross stitch, and a fly stitch rose are worked in shades of pink and mauve. To make the rose, first work an uneven number of small fly stitches in a circle. Starting in the center, weave over one spoke and under the next until the spokes are covered.

To attach the shisha mirror, position it on the fabric and outline it with small running stitches. Work a buttonhole stitch in each running stitch, then work two more rows of buttonhole stitch, one on the other and decreasing inward, to hold the mirror in place.

For the teal purse: A motif from the silk print used for the lining and strap is sewn to the front with a narrow zigzag stitch, then seed beads sewn on to cover the stitching.

❸ Place lining and outer fabric with right sides together. Stitch around the edges, using ¼ inch (.7 cm) seam allowance and leaving an 0pening of approximately 1½ inches (4 cm) at the center of one side. Trim corners and turn. Stitch the opening.

❹ Fold the lower third of the piece upward, right side out, as shown in the diagram.

❺ ***For the white purse:*** Lay an end of the cord along the open sides of the bag, cord end even with lower folded edge. Work buttonhole stitch over the cord and into the fabric, joining the bag front and back and incorporating the cord at the same time. Free the cord at the flap fold, and continue working buttonhole stitch around the outer edge of the flap.

For the teal purse: Sew a narrow fabric tube with wrong sides together. Turn right side out, pulling the cording through at the same time. (A brass tube turner speeds up this step. Make the fabric tube according to instructions with the tube.) Cut 1 inch (2.5 cm) from each end of the cording inside the tube. Turn under the fabric ends and whipstitch. Tie a knot close to each end. Whipstitch the sides of the bag together. Stitch the cord along each side seam with the knots extending slightly below the bag lower edge.

FOLD

FOLD

Embroidery By Hand

A bit of handworked embroidery provides just the finishing touch a project often needs. The stitches shown here are quick to do, and not at all difficult.

BUTTONHOLE OR BLANKET STITCH

Work the stitches close together for a buttonhole. Make them larger and space them farther apart for blanket stitch.

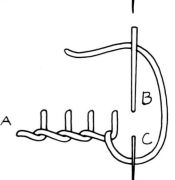

■ Bring the needle out close to the fabric edge, at A. Insert it at B and bring it out again at C, through the loop. Repeat, inserting the needle at B and bringing it out at C.

CROSS STITCH

■ To work a row of them, work the first stitch of all the crosses, then come back along the row to work the second stitch of each. The stitching goes more quickly and the results are much nicer looking.

DOUBLE CROSS STITCH

■ Work a second cross, with a vertical and a horizontal stitch, over the top of a single cross stitch.

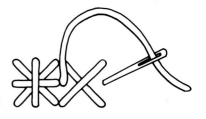

14

FRENCH KNOT

The larger the thread diameter, the larger the knot will be.

■ Bring the needle out at A. Holding the thread taut with your other hand, twist the needle twice around the thread.

■ Still holding the thread taut, insert just the point of the needle close to A.

■ Work the knot down the needle to the fabric, then push the needle through.

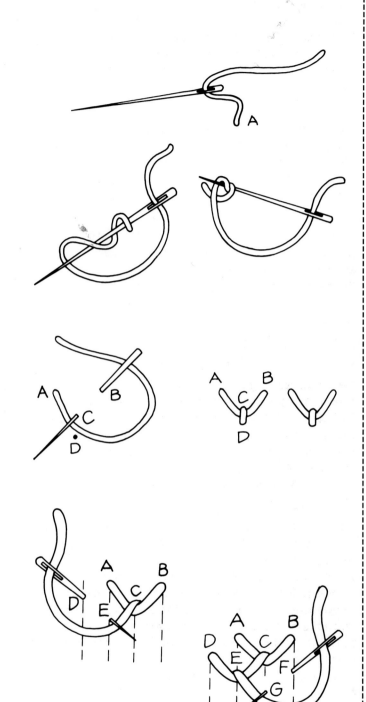

FLY STITCH

■ Bring the needle up at A. Insert it at B, leaving a slight loop, and bring it up through the loop at C. Make a straight stitch over the loop, inserting the needle at D.

FEATHER STITCH

■ Work in three imaginary columns, or draw them on the fabric to practice at first. Bring the needle out at A. Insert it at B, with the thread loop forward, and bring it up at C through the loop. Working downward, repeat the stitch at D and E. Make the next stitch below the A/B stitch, and so on.

Mixed Media Jewelry

This jewelry is about imagination! Minuscule scraps of almost anything can be included, so if your own treasure chest doesn't contain all the exotic ingredients listed below, use whatever materials you have. Consider not only fabrics, but decorative scraps of heavier paper, such as gift wrap and covers of mail order catalogs printed with good colors and designs. Incorporate materials from nature and bits of hardware. When you've made your first piece, you'll begin to look at a small piece of almost anything with an eye for its jewelry potential.

DESIGNED BY SANDY WEBSTER

Kimono Necklace

Materials

- Heavy paper or very lightweight cardboard for backing

- Synthetic suede or decorative paper for finishing the back

- Scraps of fabrics and papers with interesting texture and color

- Small beads

- 28-gauge wire

- Split rattan for edging (see step 5)

- Brush-on acrylic medium, gloss or matte finish

- High gloss acrylic spray for coating the finished piece.

- White glue

- 1 yd (1 m) decorative cord

DESIGNED BY
SANDY WEBSTER

Instructions

1. Cut a backing piece the size and shape of the kimono. Cut or tear the scraps into desired shapes and sizes. It's fun to design as you go, too.

2. Apply acrylic to the backing to "glue" the first layer of scraps in place. Thin the acrylic as necessary, according to the manufacturer's instructions. Keep it thick enough that it won't soak through the papers and fabrics. Add subsequent layers the same way.

3. Add beads or interesting buttons for ornamentation. Glue them in place, or attach them with wire, threading the wire ends though to the back of the piece and taping them.

4. Add rattan strips for edging. On the kimono pin shown, these are wrapped at intervals with wire, with the wire ends taped to the back as for the beads. You might also use stiff cord for an edging, or twigs from a woody vine.

5. When you are pleased with the design, allow the piece to dry. Then apply a coat of acrylic over the face.

6. Knot the cord approximately 2 inches (5 cm) from each end. Wrap wire around the cord just above each knot and attach it as you did the beads, just below the upper edging. Fray the ends of the cord and add beads to some of the strands, if you wish, with a knot to keep each bead in place.

7. Cut the synthetic suede to the size of the piece and glue it on the back for a neat finish.

Earrings

The earrings are made in the same way as the necklace, with a gold foil background, scraps of lightweight silk and gold lamé fabrics, and just a few beads. If desired, curve the pieces slightly while they are still damp. When the pieces are completely dry, glue on the earring backs.

Fabric and Beads

DESIGNED BY BECKY BRODERSEN

A simple fabric tube with beads inside and out makes a very versatile accessory. Wear it as a necklace, or use it to replace a ho-hum hatband. Combine several for a dramatic belt to wear over a tunic. Lengthen it to make a shoulder strap for one of the small purses shown on pages 12 and 78.

There are countless ways to combine beads and fabrics. Take along some favorite scraps when you visit a bead store and see what develops! And to entertain the kids on a slow afternoon, sew up the cloth tubes and let them add the beads.

Materials

- Fabric strip
- Beads

Instructions

Find the right combination of fabric and beads for your project. The fabric tube must be slightly larger in diameter than the beads to be used inside it, and it must slip through the holes of the beads that will be used on the outside. For fabric, try lightweight cotton, silk, or rayon.

For variety, use beads inside the tube that are a different size or shape than those on the outside. Any beads can be used inside—thrift store necklaces are a good source. Then you can splurge on really spectacular beads for the visible spots.

1. Measure the diameter of beads to be used inside the tube. Caution: There can be considerable size variance in a bag of beads that all look the same. Use the largest as a guide.

2. Add a little ease to this measurement, and add ½ inch (1 cm) for ¼-inch (.5-cm) seam allowances. Cut the fabric strip this width. For length, 39 inches (1 m) is a good average, and allows for tying the ends at the back of the neck.

3. Fold the fabric strip in half lengthwise and stitch the seam, angling each end to a point at one side and leaving an opening toward one end of the long edge for turning and inserting beads. Turn and press.

4. Mark the center of the tube with chalk or a thread loop as a guide for placement of the beads. Start and end with a bead on the outside of the tube, allowing approximately 6 inches (15 cm) at each end to tie. Then alternate a bead inside the tube with one outside, or whatever arrangement pleases you. Close the opening by hand stitching or with a small piece of fusible web.

Options

A knot in the fabric can be substituted for each external bead. Allow extra fabric length to do this.

Use a standard necklace hook (usually available where beads are sold) if it would better suit your design. Shorten the fabric tube accordingly.

Stiffened Fabric Jewelry

With scraps of pretty, lightweight fabric, fabric stiffener, and a good helping of imagination, you can create unique jewelry to suit every occasion and outfit.

Materials

- Small scraps of lightweight fabric

- Liquid fabric stiffener

- Scraps of fusible web

- For a pin, small scraps of heavy buckram or light cardboard for a backing

- Decorative beads or buttons as desired

- Jewelry findings—earring backs, pin backs, or whatever your piece requires

- White glue may be needed

Instructions

Follow the directions on the fabric stiffener container. Each kind works differently, so test it with a sample of your fabric to be sure of the results.

DESIGNED BY MARY PARKER

Crumpled Silk Pin

The pin shown in the photo begins with a 6-inch (15-cm) circle of lightweight silk. Dampen the silk with fabric stiffener, then scrunch it into the shape of a star. After the piece dries, sew a decorative gold bead at the center. Cut a piece of cardboard slightly smaller than the star and glue it on the back, then glue a bar pin to the cardboard.

Accordion-Pleated Earrings

For each earring, cut a strip of fabric 6½ inches (16.5 cm) long and ¾ inch (2 cm) wide, or to the size you prefer. Dampen it with the stiffener. At one end (the top), fuse a ¼-inch (.5-cm) double hem. Fold a narrow single hem at the other end. Then accordion-pleat the remaining section of the strip evenly and let it dry. Push the earring back through the double-hemmed end.

Necklace with Knotted Beads and Buttons

DESIGNED BY MARY PARKER

Chinese ball buttons, always popular as closures, take on a new look when strung together in a necklace. They are not difficult to make—instructions are on the next page—and can become quite addictive when you begin to experiment with different fabrics.

This necklace is 33 inches (84 cm) long, made to slip over the head without a closure.

Materials

For each small bead:

- Fabric strip ¾ inch (2.5 cm) wide, approximately 10 inches (25.5 cm) long

- Cotton cording, 10-inch (25.5-cm) length, ⅛ inch (.3 cm) diameter

For each large bead:

- Fabric strip 1 inch (2.5 cm) wide, approximately 12 inches (30.5 cm) long

- Cotton cording, ¼ inch (6 mm) diameter, one piece for each bead

- For spacer at necklace back, an additional 4-inch (10-cm) fabric strip and length of cording

- Buttons or disk beads: 14, ⅝ inch (1.5 cm) diameter; 6, ¾ inch (2 cm); 8, ⅞ inch (2.3 cm); 8, 1 inch (2.5 cm)

- Heavy thread, topstitching or buttonhole weight, for stringing beads

- Tube turners. The most useful kind is a set of sturdy hollow metal tubes in varying sizes. A spiral-tipped wire is used to pull the fabric tube right side out through the metal tube and to insert cording at the same time. If this kind of turner is used, modify fabric strip widths according to the manufacturer's instructions.

Instructions

Make a total of 31 knotted beads. Make 17 large and 14 small, or include some intermediate sizes if you like.

1 Sew fabric strips to make tubes. Follow instructions with the tube turners, or sew long edges, right sides together, with ¼ inch (.7 cm) seam allowance. Turn; insert the cording.

Tip: For faster results, sew the longest strips that can be turned right side out easily, then cut into individual lengths after inserting the cord.

2 Make the knotted beads. Save one corded length, approximately 4 inches (10 cm) to use as the spacer at the back of the necklace.

3 Arrange the beads. Begin with a large one at the center front of the necklace and grade to smaller sizes at the back. Place one or two buttons between each pair of beads, grading the sizes in the same way.

4 Thread a needle with strong thread somewhat longer than the planned necklace length.

5 Leaving several inches of thread tail, work the needle through the spacer first, between the fabric and the cord. Then sew through the center of each knot and through each bead or button, keeping the best side of each toward the front of the necklace. Leave a thread tail. Repeat twice more, knot all the thread ends together securely and hide the knot inside the spacer. Turn under the fabric at the ends of the spacer and stitch them in place.

Chinese Ball Buttons

These intricate-looking knots are often used as closures on traditional oriental garments. They are such fun to make you will soon be inventing new ways to use them.

Once you have mastered the weaving sequence, try a few variations: For a double knot, follow the same weaving sequence a second time. Repeat once more to make a triple knot. You can obtain some interesting effects, too, by working two colors or textures of fine cord together.

The knots can be made of purchased decorative cord or from a corded fabric tube as was used for the necklace above. The thickness of the cord will determine the finished size of the knot. The length of cord you will need for each knot depends upon the cord diameter: For ⅛ inch (3 mm) cord, cut a piece approximately 8 inches (20 cm) long; for ½ inch (1.3 cm) cord, cut approximately 15 inches (38 cm). For your first attempts, it is easier to work with a longer piece of cord; when you've tried a few you may find you can cut the cord shorter.

If you are working with corded fabric tubes, keep the seam to the underside as you form the knot. Don't allow the tube to twist.

(continued on following page)

Chinese Ball Buttons *(continued from previous page)*

TO MAKE EACH KNOT:

1 Form a loop toward one end of the cord.

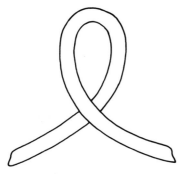

2 Form a second loop behind the first, and place the second cord end over the first.

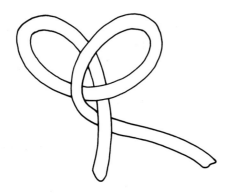

3 Weave the right (first) end in and out of the loops.

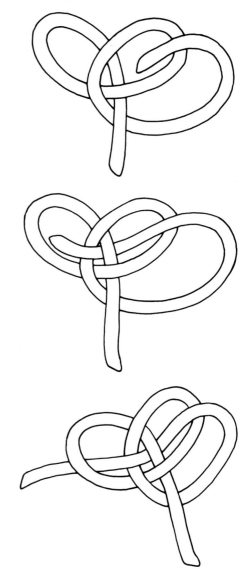

4 Pull the ends to tighten.

5 Cut off all but ½ inch (1 cm) of the excess length at each end. Cut away this same length of the inside cord from each end.

6 Fold the raw ends together and hand stitch to the underside of the knot.

Silk Fabric Pins

DESIGNED BY MARY PARKER

Vibrant suit-weight silks are accented with silk yarn to make these colorful pins. Search your own scrap basket for interesting combinations of color and texture. Try this technique for earrings, too! The pins illustrated are 2 inches (5 cm) square.

Materials

- Small scraps of heavy silk or other fabric with good texture, two different colors

- Scraps of yarn

- Decorative bead or button, if desired

- Invisible thread or a color to harmonize with yarn, for couching

- Medium weight non-corrugated cardboard, a 2-inch (5-cm) square

- Bar pin

- White glue

- Fusible web, small pieces

Instructions

❶ Cut a 3½-inch (9-cm) square of fabric for the background. For the foreground, cut a 2-inch (5-cm) square. If you like, add an additional layer as on the green and aqua pin—just cut one more piece, 1½ inches (4 cm) square.

❷ Press edges of the smaller square ¼ inch (.7 cm) to the wrong side. Cut away a notch at each corner so the fabric will lie flat.

❸ Center the smaller square on the right side of the larger one and fuse the two together.

❹ Arrange yarn on top, in whatever pattern you like, keeping ¾ inch (2 cm) from the outer edges. Couch the yarn to the fabric by stitching over it with a zigzag stitch wide enough to straddle the yarn. As an alternative, glue the yarn to the fabric.

❺ Spread a thin layer of glue over one side of the cardboard and let it dry until slightly tacky. Center the cardboard on the wrong side of the fabric piece and press in place. Clip a notch in the fabric margin at each corner. Turn the piece fabric side down and spread glue along the edges of the back; press the fabric edges to the wrong side.

❻ Arrange more yarn strands to extend from one or two edges of the pin and glue them to the back. Stitch a decorative bead or button at the lower corner, if desired. Glue the bar pin in place on the back.

After you have sewn up a pile of patchwork pillows for every room, how can you incorporate small fabric leftovers into the decorating scheme? Here are a few suggestions that may help you think of dozens more.

Shimmery Basket

DESIGNED BY ANNE McCLOSKEY

Always handy for storing this and that, an attractive basket can add sparkle to a dull corner of a room. This one combines scraps of silky-finish fabrics in jewel tones, wound around a rope core. We have used mostly solid colors, but try a variety of patterned fabrics for an altogether different effect. Varying the length of the fabric strips produces an interesting overall pattern. The finished basket is 8 inches (20 cm) high, exclusive of handle, and 14 inches (35.5 cm) in diameter.

Materials

- Scraps of solid-colored and patterned fabrics cut into cross-grain strips approximately 2½ to 3 inches (6 to 8 cm) wide and varying in length

- 12 yds (11 m) soft roping, 1½ inch (3.8 cm) diameter

- Invisible thread or decorative thread for joining coils

- Assorted scrap yarns to decorate the basket handle

- Tacky glue

Instructions

1 Thread a hand sewing needle with decorative or invisible thread and have it ready.

2 Working on a flat surface, fold the end of one fabric strip over the end of the roping and glue it in place. Wrap the fabric strip around the roping diagonally, overlapping by about 1 inch (2.5 cm) with each wrap. Wind the fabric fairly tightly. Cover approximately 12 inches (30 cm) of roping this way, then make a coil to form the bottom of the basket, keeping the end of the roping at the center.

3 Coil one or two rounds, then stitch the coils together by hand.

4 Each time a new fabric strip is added, glue the end of the old strip and beginning of the new one to the roping.

5 Work until the bottom measures approximately 14 inches (35.5 cm) across, stitch it, then start up the sides. Place the next round directly on top of the previous one, and stitch them together after each layer is added. You can make the sides straight, or shape them as you wish.

6 When the sides are the desired height, stitch the covered rope securely in place at one side and loop the next section over the top of the basket to create a handle. Cover the end with fabric and stitch it in place on the opposite side.

7 Twist or braid strands of yarn to decorate the handle. Wind them around and knot at one end to make a tassel.

Fabric-Covered Recipe Box

Nearly every household has one of those metal boxes sized to hold three-by-five cards. No one remembers where it came from. Through its long life it has housed a variety of objects—perhaps even three-by-five cards. It is invariably one of those grayish green military surplus colors. It is a useful thing, and can quickly be dressed up with some creative scrap-crafting. These boxes are still available inexpensively from discount and office supply stores. The same technique, of course, can be used to decorate any box with a hinged lid. This is a good project to use up scraps that are too small for anything else. Almost any kind of material can be used as long as it is not so thin that the glue seeps through.

DESIGNED BY XANATH ESPINA

Materials

- File box
- Fabric scraps
- White glue
- Water-based polyurethane finish and appropriate brush

Instructions

1 If the box is an old one, make sure the surface is clean. Sand lightly to rough up the finish so fabric will adhere well.

2 If desired, trim edges of fabrics cleanly, or pink them.

3 Apply glue to a small area of the box. Use a small piece of stiff cardboard to spread the glue evenly. Allow it to dry a moment so it is slightly tacky, and position the fabric pieces. Apply a thin coat of glue to fabric scrap on the box where another piece will overlap. Arrange scraps so they wrap around corners of the box and lid, but with edges of the scraps even with open edges of the box and lid so as not to interfere with the box closing properly. When the entire surface of the box is covered, let it dry thoroughly.

4 Following the manufacturer's instructions, apply the finish. Use three or four coats for best protection, allowing adequate drying time in between.

Reversible Place Mats

The advantage of this place mat design is that no two mats need be the same. If you want some continuity, you might use the same fabric for the face side of all the mats in your set, then use a different fabric for the reverse side of each one. Or cut the edging squares for all the mats from the same fabric.

DESIGNED BY BIRD ROSS

Materials

For each mat:

- Fabric for upper side

- Fabric for reverse side

- Fabric for an inner layer, to add stability to light-weight outer fabrics

- Assorted fabrics to bind edges

- Plenty of thread

Instructions

1 Determine the finished size for your mat; 12 by 16 inches (30.5 by 40.5 cm) is standard. Cut fabrics for front, reverse, and inner layers slightly larger than the planned finished size.

2 Cut squares to bind the edges. You will need approximately 36 3½-inch (9-cm) squares.

3 Assemble and stitch the mat according to the instructions on pages 30 and 31. It is especially important to machine wash and dry the mats before the edging is applied so they will lie flat.

Zigzag Quilting

Designer Bird Ross has developed a distinctive manual zigzag technique that combines fabric scraps in a uniquely artistic way. The process itself is wonderfully entertaining and therapeutic too! It's a great means of using up not only fabric scraps, but all those odd-colored spools of thread with just a few yards remaining.

The technique involves making a fabric "sandwich" of two or three layers, then machine-quilting the pieces together, stitching over the entire surface in a random zigzag pattern. The edges are then bound with small cloth squares that are overlapped and stitched in place.

Part of the technique's charm is the softly frayed look of the pieces, best obtained with light- to medium-weight cotton and linen fabrics. Experiment with combinations of colors, patterns, and textures to see what pleases your eye. If your project calls for a stabilizing layer between the two outer fabrics, choose a firm, lightweight cotton fabric. Preshrink all the fabrics before you begin.

For the stitching, use harmonizing or contrasting thread colors. Frequent color changes in both needle and bobbin make the piece interesting.

Practice the stitching technique on scraps first. It can feel a bit awkward until you are accustomed to the freedom of it.

It is a good idea to use a larger size machine needle with this technique. There is a considerable amount of stitching involved, and toward the end you will be sewing through many layers of fabric. Try a sharp or "jeans" needle, and change it midway through the project.

MAKE THE FABRIC SANDWICH

1. Cut face and reverse fabrics for the central portion of the project. Cut these slightly larger than the intended finished size of the article because the dense stitching will cause the fabric to draw up somewhat. In addition, this will allow you to trim the edges evenly if the layers have shifted during stitching.

2. If a thicker finished fabric is preferred, also cut an inner layer the same size from a stable, lightweight fabric that is compatible with the outer fabrics.

3. Sandwich the fabric layers right side out with the stabilizing fabric, if used, between them. Pin baste them together at intervals.

4. Now stitch the layers together. Set the machine for a medium-length straight stitch. Sew a few inches forward, turn slightly, and sew a few inches in reverse. Change stitching direction every 6 to 10 inches (15 to 25 cm) or so. Continue until the whole piece is lightly covered with stitching. If the layers seem to be shifting badly, try a walking foot or even-feed foot, and/or stitch more slowly.

5. Stitch all over the piece again, changing both needle and bobbin thread colors, if you wish. Then repeat this step once more.

6. Wash and dry the piece. Steam press to make it lie flat. Trim to even up the edges if necessary, and trim away long thread ends.

ADD THE EDGING

1 Determine the size of the individual squares for edging. Larger ones, up to 4 or 5 inches (10 to 12 cm), look best on a larger piece such as a table mat; for a place mat, cut them 1½ to 2 inches (3 to 5 cm). Calculate the number you will need by arranging a few along the edge of the fabric as shown. Cut the fabric squares.

2 To save time, stack the edging squares at the right side of the sewing machine in the order they will be used.

3 Beginning along a straight edge, place a square diagonally half on and half off the edge of the fabric as shown. Stitch it in place, stitching in a zigzag pattern to catch the edge of the square to the main fabric. Do a minimal amount of stitching at this point; you will stitch over each square again on the other side.

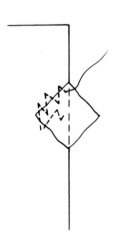

4 Stop stitching about halfway along and position the second piece as shown.

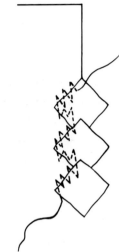

5 When you reach a corner, it is easiest to place place a square as shown.

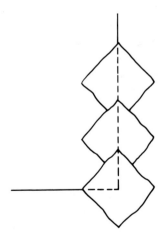

6 When all the edging squares are in place, turn the piece over, fold the squares over the fabric edge, and stitch again in the same way. At each corner, fold the square in half over the edge, then fold to miter the corner smoothly.

Ribbon-Trimmed Bulletin Board

DESIGNED BY SUSAN KINNEY

Materials

- Fiberboard piece, or two pieces of foamcore glued together
- Lengths of ribbon or narrow decorative trim
- Fabric
- Fusible fiberfill batting
- Staple gun, or duct tape
- Small screw eyes
- Picture wire

Instructions

1 Cut fiberboard or foamcore to the desired size for the base. Cut two pieces of batting this same size. Cut fabric (or piece it) large enough to wrap over the edges of the base with approximately 1 inch (2.5 cm) margin all around.

2 Fuse one batting layer to the other, then fuse the two to the board. They only need to stick well enough to hold them in place temporarily.

3 Smooth the fabric over the batting with even margins around all edges. Pull it to the back of the base and tape or staple in place. In order to get the fabric evenly taut, attach at the corners first, then the center of each side. Then tape or staple halfway between the previously placed staples, and so on.

4 Cut lengths of ribbon as you go, and stretch them diagonally over the face of the padded board, keeping them taut. Staple or tape securely on the back. Add more ribbons in the opposite direction, as shown in the photo.

5 Neaten the back, if desired, by gluing a large sheet of paper or other fabric to cover all the staples.

6 Attach a screw eye approximately one-third of the way down from the top on each side of the back. Attach wire for hanging.

With ribbons or lengths of decorative cord to hold the papers in place, no pushpins are needed! Use plain fabric and an assortment of patterned ribbons, or a patterned fabric with ribbons to pick up its colors.

Switch Cover Art

You can, of course, just glue fabric over an ordinary light switch or outlet cover and instantly improve its appearance, but why not go a step further and embellish the fabric a little first? For ours, tiny fabric squares, a length of interesting fringed selvage, and a few bone beads were used as accents on a natural linen background. Try machine embroidery with several different thread colors, or miniature patchwork, or perhaps an appliquéd motif. Your artwork will make an unusual housewarming gift!

Materials

- Switch or outlet cover

- Sandpaper

- Fabric

- Embellishments

- Dry adhesive sheet, available at art supply stores

- Liquid fray retardant

Instructions

❶ Cut the base fabric approximately ⅝ inch (1.5 cm) larger all around than the switch cover and add the desired decorations.

❷ Peel off the protective cover from the adhesive sheet (follow the instructions on the package) and press it to the back of the fabric.

❸ Sand the face of the cover lightly to rough up the surface so the adhesive will adhere better. Wipe it thoroughly.

❹ Remove the backing from the fabric piece and press onto the cover. Press the fabric edges to the back, cutting away excess at the corners for a smooth fit. From the back, poke a hole at the center of the switch opening and carefully clip almost to each corner. Press the resulting fabric triangles to the back. Apply a drop of fray retardant at each corner if necessary. Poke through the fabric at the screw hole positions. Trim frayed threads and apply fray retardant if it's needed.

❺ As a precaution, switch off the circuit breaker before putting the new cover in place.

Thunderstorm Wreath

Clouds, lightning bolts, and crystal droplets bring the illusion of a cooling rain to steamy summer days. The wreath is quick to assemble and makes a clever gift for your vacation hostess.

Materials and Tools

- ½ yard (.5 m) white cotton organdy, 45 inches (114 cm) wide

- ⅜ yard (.35 m) silver tricot lamé, 45 inches (114 cm) wide

- 13-inch (33-cm) macramé ring

- Fiberfill or other stuffing

- 25 crystal beads, 8 mm diameter

- Metallic silver sewing thread

- Blue-gray crayon or powder eye shadow

- Dressmaker's tracing paper and wheel

DESIGNED BY DEE DEE TRIPLETT

Instructions

1 Enlarge the pattern pieces.

2 Fold the white fabric in half wrong side out. Trace seven cloud shapes, allowing approximately ½ inch (1.5 cm) space between them. Stitch around the shapes before cutting them out, leaving an opening between marks for turning. Cut around the shapes, leaving ⅛ inch (3 mm) seam allowance. Clip corners and curves and turn right side out.

3 Shade the cloud curves with crayon or eye shadow to suggest clouds heavy with rain. Stuff lightly and close the openings.

4 Make three lightning bolts the same way from the silver fabric.

5 Assemble the wreath. Arrange the clouds on the face of the ring, overlapping them slightly. Pin them to the ring and to each other. Whip clouds to the ring, and tack them invisibly to each other.

34

Arrange the lightning bolts to suggest a bow. Tack them invisibly to the clouds.

6 Add beads for the raindrops. Thread beads onto the silver metallic thread as shown, tying the beads at about 1-inch (2.5 cm) intervals. Stitch the strands to clouds at the top of the ring and let them dangle loosely to suggest raindrops.

Thunderstorm Wreath

Seam allowances not included—see instructions
Patterns are 50% of actual size

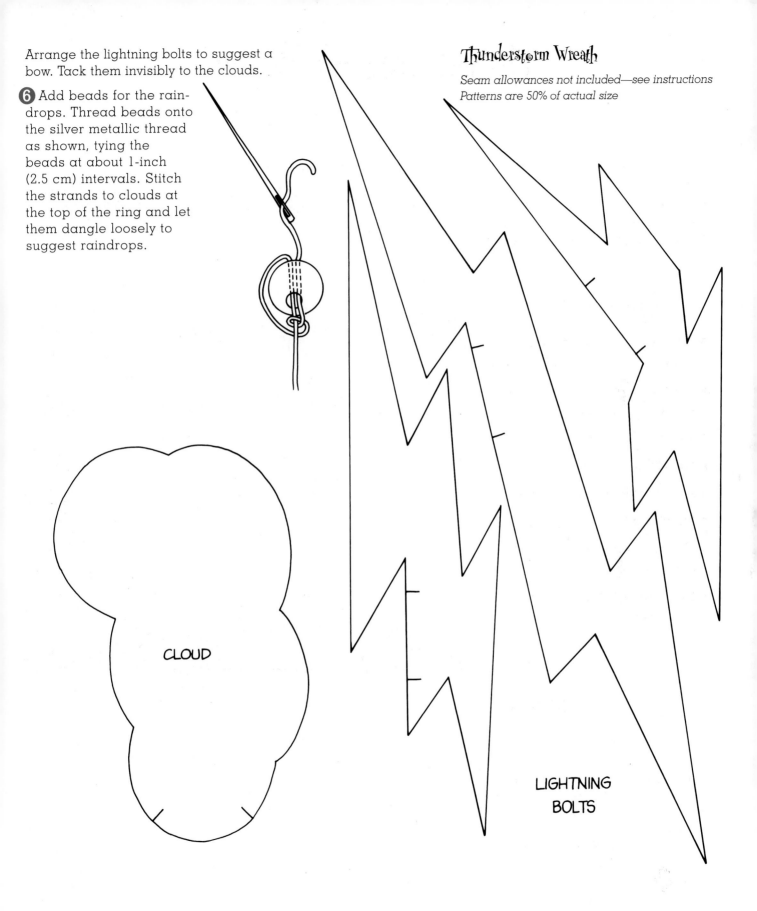

CLOUD

LIGHTNING BOLTS

Table Mat

This charming table cover doubles as a handy picnic cloth, too. Since it's reversible, you might make one side of flamboyant colors and patterns for everyday use, and the other in a more subtle color scheme for use on auspicious occasions. We've used just one fabric for the central portion of the mat, but this section, too, could be pieced to incorporate more patterns and textures.

DESIGNED BY
BIRD ROSS

Materials

- Fabric for mat front and squares to cover seams
- Fabric for mat reverse si···s and squares to cover seams
- Fabric for inner stabilizing lay·r
- Contrast fabric for inner borde·

- Second contrast fabric for edging squares
- Plenty of thread

Instructions

This mat is made according to the instructions on pages 30 and 31, except that it is made in four sections for handling ease. An additional border pattern of small squares has been added to one side.

1 On a piece of paper, draw a rectangle to indicate the finished size of your cloth. Divide it into even fourths. Add 3 inches (7.5 cm) to each side of each piece.

2 Cut four pieces the above size from the front, reverse, and inner fabrics.

3 Sandwich and stitch the layers according to the instructions on page 30.

4 Cut contrast squares for the inner border on the cloth front. These may be slightly larger or smaller than the edging squares, or the same size. You will need quite a few of them—cut a dozen or so and lay them out to determine the total number.

5 Position these squares in an overlapping pattern to create an inner border along two adjacent edges of each rectangle. Stitch one, then overlap with the next, and so on, catching the edges of each and sewing with the same random zigzag pattern. Remember the edging squares will be added later.

6 Machine wash and dry the pieces.

7 Square off the inner (unbordered) edges of each piece. Trim only the inner fabric layer. Place two adjacent quarters together on a table, making sure edges of their inner layers abut. Overlap the two outer layers and the two reverse side layers slightly. Join them with a straight stitch seam. Repeat this with the other pair of quarters.

8 Cut squares of the face and reverse fabrics to cover the seams on both sides of each piece. These may be the same size as the inner border squares, or slightly different. Working first on the face side then on the reverse side, sew the squares over the seamline in the same way you did the border.

9 Trim and stitch the two halves and sew squares over the seamline on both sides.

10 Add the edging squares as described on page 31.

Jeans Quilt

DESIGNED BY BRENDA SCONYERS

If your attic contains a box full of jeans your kids have outgrown through the years, here is a great way to use them up. Send each child off to college with a warm quilt that also serves as a remembrance of childhood days.

Materials

- Assorted old jeans—denim skirts and jackets too
- Batting
- Backing fabric

Instructions

See page 41 for tips on sewing heavy fabrics without frustration.

1 Determine the finished size of the quilt. Calculate the number of squares needed to make up the top. Remember to include seam allowance; for thick fabric like this denim, add ⅜ inch (1 cm) at each side.

2 Cut the denim squares. Make use of the design features: zippers, pockets, patches, designer labels, and even holes that commemorate special events.

3 Sew the squares with right sides together to form strips. Press the seams, then sew the strips together.

4 Baste the batting to the top, stitching just outside the seamline. Trim batting to the stitching.

5 Sew the top and backing with right sides together, leaving an opening for turning. Trim the corners and turn right side out.

6 To join the layers securely, stitch along selected seamlines or around some design lines on the right side of the quilt.

Photo Album Cover

A truly devoted scrap-saver is reluctant to throw away even the miles of trimmings created by a serger-sewn project. Finding a use for them is challenging! Here they are used to decorate a photo album, glued over a three-dimensional papier-mâché form to add marvelous texture and depth.

As this album was created to hold a vast collection of pictures of the family dog, the designer chose a stylized dog shape for the papier-mâché figures. She created her own shape, but any inexpensive plastic toy or household object can serve as a mold.

Materials

- Photo album
- Serger scraps in bright and dark colors
- Fabric remnant, 1 inch (2.5 cm) larger all around than total size of album cover
- Decorative paper or fabric for endsheets, 2 pieces the size of the covers
- Instant papier-mâché, or paper strips and wheat paste to make your own
- Form for papier-mâché figure
- White fabric glue
- Beads, buttons, or shells for accent
- Small, fairly stiff paintbrush

DESIGNED BY
FLETA MONAGHAN

Instructions

1 From papier-mâché, make a three-dimensional form with one flat side. Allow it to dry thoroughly.

2 With the small paintbrush and white glue, glue serger strips over the form to completely cover all but the flat side. Use the bright, light colors for raised areas and dark strips for recessed areas so the design will stand out. Apply glue sparingly so that it doesn't soak through the fabric.

3 Iron the large piece of fabric well. Outline the album cover—front, spine, and back—on the wrong side.

4 Brush glue over entire outer surface of the album and scrape off excess with a piece of cardboard. Too much glue will bleed through the fabric.

5 Carefully place the glued album within the outline on the fabric. Turn the piece over and smooth out any wrinkles, trying not to stretch the fabric. Trim away excess fabric, leaving a 1-inch (2.5-cm) margin around the edges.

6 Make a diagonal clip at each corner, cutting to within ¼ inch (.5 cm) of the cover corner.

7 Spread a thin coating of glue along the cover edges, and ¾ inch (2 cm) or so to the inside of the cover. Fold in the fabric at each corner. Brush the corner fabric very lightly with glue and fold in remaining edges of fabric.

8 On the album front, position and glue the scrap-covered figure.

9 Glue more serger strips around the figures, if desired, and glue buttons, shells, or other decorative objects here and there.

10 Cut decorative paper sheets slightly smaller than the covers and glue inside the front and back covers.

Sewing Heavy Fabrics

Most sewing problems associated with very heavy fabrics such as denim—broken needles, uneven stitching—can be avoided simply by assuring that the presser foot rides evenly over the fabric. If feed dogs are in contact with the fabric only under one side of the foot, or there is a much greater thickness of fabric under either the front or back of the foot, the fabric cannot feed evenly. Stitching is uneven, or the fabric won't feed at all without pushing and tugging at it.

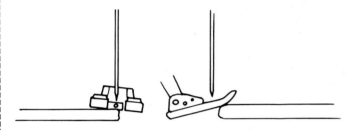

Make a little "hitchhiker" by folding a small piece of the same fabric to the same number of thicknesses as you are sewing. When sewing along, and close to, an edge, place the hitchhiker under the other side of the presser foot.

As you approach a corner, place it under the front of the foot. Then pivot at the corner with the needle down, and place it under the back of the foot for a few stitches, then move it to the side again.

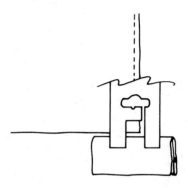

Use this method, too, when sewing across a heavy seam. Place the hitchhiker under the back of the foot to prevent the foot tilting uphill at the seam. Take a few stitches, then put it under the front of the foot to prevent a downhill tilt. Take care not to stitch through the hitchhiker when using it under the front of the presser foot.

A special "jeans" presser foot is available for some machines. It is a straight stitch foot with a beveled edge around the needle hole to deflect the needle and prevent breakage.

Needles make a difference too. Needles designated as "jeans" needles have sharp points for easy penetration of dense fabric. With the slightly rounded "universal" point of a standard needle, the needle can hit a tough fiber in the fabric and will bend or break rather than slide through. Jeans needles are made in larger sizes—90/14 to 120/20.

Silk Marquetry

DESIGNED BY PAT SCHEIBLE

The craft of marquetry is most often associated with wood, with the colors and textures of different woods combined to create an intricate design or picture. The same technique applied to fabric can produce some fascinating results, almost like non-sewn quilting.

For fabric marquetry, fabric pieces are backed with adhesive, cut to shape, then mounted on board with the edges abutted. The technique is as effective for abstract designs as it is for realistic portraits. We have used scraps of lightweight silk in small patterns and solid colors, but most any lightweight fabric would work.

DESIGNED BY PAT SCHEIBLE

To copy a photograph in fabric, it may be helpful to first make a black and white photocopy so you can more easily distinguish light, dark, and intermediate shades. Then choose fabrics to represent the color values and to add texture where you want it.

Materials

- Fabric scraps
- Dry adhesive sheets (available at art supply stores)
- Your design or photo
- Mat board
- Very sharp scissors
- Fine point marker
- Burnishing tool

Instructions

Refer also to the instructions that accompany the dry adhesive sheets.

1. Enlarge or reduce the photo or design so it is the desired finished size. Divide up the design into individual sections to be cut from different fabrics.

2. Trace the design sections, in reverse, onto the adhesive sheet backing and cut out the sections.

3. Lightly outline the design on the mat board. As you position fabric sections onto the board, work from the center of the design outward.

4. Remove the protective overlay sheet and smooth each design section to the back of the corresponding fabric. Carefully trim away excess fabric, remove the backing, and place the adhesive-backed fabric in position on the mat board. Use the burnisher to smooth it into place. If you need to reposition a piece, peel it gently off the board and remount it without reapplying adhesive.

Special Occasions

It's fun to commemorate not just the holidays, but special events in the lives of friends and family members. A small gift can be sewn up quickly and will be remembered for a long time.

One-of-a-Kind Note Cards

DESIGNED BY TERRY TAYLOR

Express your best wishes with a greeting card designed just for the occasion. For a truly special gift, make up an assortment of designs and tie them with a ribbon.

We have used silk from flea market neckties for several of these cards and embellished them with embroidery, using metallic and silk threads as well as conventional cotton (for stitches, see page 14). Accents are from old costume jewelry. Once you've made a few cards, you'll find ways to incorporate all sorts of fabrics, paper scraps, and flat ornamental pieces in your own creations.

The designs shown in the photo, clockwise from left, are: Heart in Hand, Beret, Crazy Patchwork, Geometric Exercise, Stars and Strips, Autumn Leaves, and Golden Grid.

Materials

- Blank note cards with envelopes
- Scraps of lightweight fabrics, solids and small patterns
- Paper-backed fusible web
- Assorted embroidery threads, including silk and metallic
- White glue
- Craft knife with sharp blade
- Small sheets of plain or ornamental paper

Instructions

If your design produces a messy "wrong side," glue on a small sheet of decorative paper to cover the back of the work.

Heart in Hand, Autumn Leaves, Geometric Exercise

❶ Trace shapes, in reverse, on the paper side of the fusible web. Fuse according to the manufacturer's instructions, and cut out the shapes.

❷ Fuse the shapes to the cards.

❸ Accent the card with straight and cross stitches as desired. Knot the thread ends on the back and secure with a tiny drop of white glue.

Beret

Wool or felt scraps work well for this design.

❶ Cut three concentric circles of wool or felt. Work blanket stitch around the edges of the largest circle with metallic thread.

❷ Pin the medium-sized circle to the larger one and blanket stitch around the edge, catching to the larger circle. Pin the smallest circle to the other two and attach it with blanket stitch.

❸ Accent the circles with feather, lazy daisy, or other embroidery stitches.

❹ Glue the circles to the card. Press with a heavy book until dry.

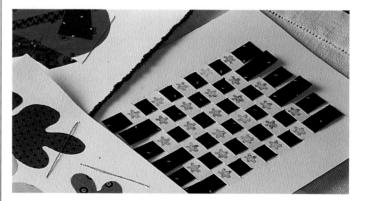

Stars and Strips

For this design you will also need a pencil with an unused eraser to make the stamp, and a stamp pad with metallic gold ink.

❶ On the front of the card, lightly draw a rectangle that is evenly divisible on both sides by 1/2 inch (1.5 cm).

2 In the rectangle, draw horizontal lines ½ inch (1.5 cm) apart. Cut along the lines with a sharp craft knife.

3 Fuse a fabric scrap the size of the rectangle with paper backed web.

4 Cut the backed fabric into ½-inch (1.5-cm) strips. Do not peel away the paper.

5 Weave the fabric strips through the card as illustrated.

6 To make a stamp, lightly draw the star outline on the pencil eraser. Carefully cut around the outline, first cutting straight down with the blade then removing the excess around the shape.

7 Stamp the design in the negative spaces on the woven card.

8 If necessary, glue the ends of the fabric strips in place.

Crazy Patchwork

1 Mark a rectangle on the front of the card for the patchwork.

2 Draw a rectangle the same size on the paper side of the fusible web. Within this rectangle, draw shapes for the patchwork pieces.

3 Cut the web apart on the lines and fuse to fabric pieces.

4 Fuse the scraps to the card, carefully aligning edges.

5 Accent the "seams" with feather, blanket, straight, or other decorative stitches as desired.

6 For further accent, glue on flat jewelry components or other treasures. Press the card under a heavy book until the glue dries.

Golden Grid

1 On the fusible web backing, mark off a rectangle the size of the design area on the card. Cut, and fuse to fabric.

2 Cut out the backed rectangle and fuse it to the card.

3 Mark the edges of the rectangle at equidistant intervals of approximately ⅜ inch (1 cm).

4 Thread a needle with a long piece of metallic thread and knot the end.

5 Starting at the lower right corner of the rectangle, bring the thread up from the back of the card at the first mark and make a diagonal stitch to corresponding mark at the opposite corner.

6 Continue making long straight stitches between diagonally opposite marks.

7 When stitching is finished in one direction, rethread the needle and work stitches in the other direction, weaving them in and out of the first stitches if desired.

8 Add an accent at the center. Glue it in place, then press the card under a heavy book until dry.

Picnic Tote and Woven Mats

DESIGNED BY MARY PARKER

The bag's colorful stripes are actually pieced strips of fabric, stitched decoratively along the seamlines. The tote is roomy enough—and sturdy enough—to carry all the picnic essentials for several hungry people. In the off-season, it doubles as a very practical carry-all.

On our model, decorative stitching was worked with ribbon floss on a serger, but the design of the bag allows for all sorts of creative embellishment. Try a favorite machine embroidery stitch and any decorative thread.

The finished size of the bag is 17½ inches (44 cm) wide, 16 inches (40.5 cm) high, 6 inches (15 cm) deep.

Picnic Tote

- Assorted fabric scraps to make 44 strips, each 17 inches (43 cm) long and 1½ inches (4 cm) wide

- Heavier fabric for handles: 4 strips, 54 inches (137 cm) long and 1½ inches (4 cm) wide

- Handle lining fabric: 4 strips, 26 inches long and 1½ inches (4 cm) wide

- Lining fabric, 48 by 17 inches (122 cm by 43 cm)

- Fusible fleece, 48 by 16 inches (122 cm by 40.5 cm)

- Decorative threads as desired. We used three spools of ribbon floss, sewing thread to match, and one spool of invisible thread.

- Roll of fusible web, ¾ inch (2 cm) wide

Optional but handy:

- 25 mm bias tape maker

Instructions

It is easiest to plan the tote by laying out all the fabric strips first on a long table or long stretch of floor space. Use the diagram on page 50 as a guide, and place the handles in position as shown.

Assemble the handles.

❶ Fold under and press ¼ inch (.7 cm) along the long edges of handle and lining strips. To speed up this step, draw the strip through the tape maker and press the folds as you go. With wrong sides together, center a lining strip lengthwise against each handle strip. Use a strip of fusible web to bond the two together.

Note: With the lightweight fabrics for this bag, the folds at the handle edges add strength. If very heavy fabric is used for the handles, the handle and lining pieces can be joined with a decorative serger seam, the seam allowances trimmed off at the same time.

❷ To finish the handles with the serger and ribbon floss as illustrated: Set up the serger for a two-thread overlock. Thread the looper with ribbon floss and use matching thread in the left needle. Shorten the stitch length for an attractive satin stitch, and adjust the tension so that the floss stitching curls slightly over the fabric edge.

❸ As an alternative, finish the handle edges with a machine embroidery stitch or overcast stitch and decorative thread.

Assemble the tote.

❶ Begin at the left edge of section A as shown in the layout on page 50. Sew the first two strips along the long edges with right sides together and ¼ inch (.7 cm) seam allowance. Add the next strip and subsequent strips in the same way to complete section A. Press seams open.

❷ Join strips to construct sections B, C, D, and E the same way.

❸ Lay out the fleece, fusible side up. Place pieced section A, right side up with fabric strips vertical, at the left side of the fleece with the left edges aligned and the upper and lower edges of the pieced section extending ½ inch (1.3 cm) above and below the fleece. Fuse the pieces according to the manufacturer's instructions.

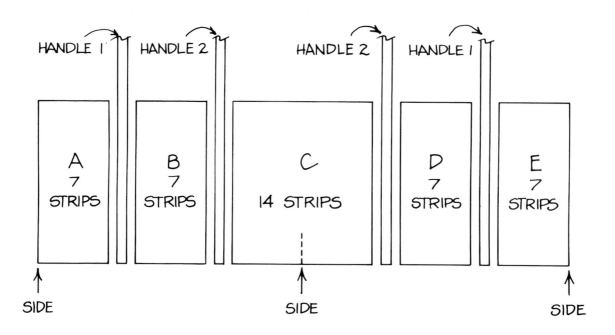

HANDLE 1　HANDLE 2　　HANDLE 2　HANDLE 1

A
7
STRIPS

B
7
STRIPS

C
14 STRIPS

D
7
STRIPS

E
7
STRIPS

SIDE　　　　　　SIDE　　　　　　SIDE

4 Position the first handle strip next to section A so that the finished edge of the handle overlaps the raw edge of section A by ¼ inch (.7 cm) and unfinished handle end is even with the lower edge of the fabric piece. Position pieced section B on the fleece, slipping ¼ inch (.7 cm) at the unfinished side under the handle and aligning the upper and lower edges with section A. Fuse these two pieces to the fleece.

5 Position the second handle and section C as above, and fuse. Bring the free end of handle 2 down in a U to align with the lower edge of the piece so that the handle edge overlaps the right edge of piece C. Then position section D, slipping it under the other handle edge. Fuse these pieces.

6 Position the free end of handle 1 and section E and fuse them in the same way.

7 Embellish the seamlines as desired. On the model tote, invisible thread was used to couch ribbon floss along the seams. To do this, set the machine for a medium to wide zigzag stitch at a moderate stitch length. Stitch over the floss, guiding it so the zigzag stitches straddle it but the needle doesn't pierce it. (A cording presser foot or any foot with a center groove is helpful for couching.)

8 Fold the piece in half with right sides together, aligning the unfinished ends and lower edges. Stitch lower edge, stitching only 7¼ inches (18.5 cm) out from center in each direction. There will be an opening of 4¾ inch (12 cm) at each end. Press the seam open. Topstitch ¼ inch (.7 cm) from the seamline on each side to reinforce the seam.

9 With the tote wrong side out, bring the open edges at one end of the tote together so that the bottom seam is centered on one side. Sew these edges together. Repeat on the other end.

Add the lining.

1 Fold the lining in half wrong side out, the short edges together. Using ¼ inch (.7 cm) seam allowance, sew the lower 7 inches (18 cm) and upper 2 inches (5 cm) of the end seam.

2 With the tote right side out and the handles folded down to the right side, slip the lining over the tote, aligning the end seamlines. Stitch together along the upper edge. Stop when you reach each handle and backstitch securely, then resume stitching the other side of the handle.

3 Sew the bottom of the lining as on the tote itself (steps 12 and 13). Turn right side out through the opening in the lining. Press lining seam allowances to the inside at the handles and whipstitch or topstitch the openings.

The reversible mats are constructed of interwoven strips to provide built-in holders for utensils. When it's picnic time, just add the napkins, roll up the mats and tie them with the self ties, then toss them into the matching tote. Use them at home to brighten up a meal at the backyard picnic table.

The back is a solid piece of fabric, and the mat is edged all around with bias binding. The finished size is 19 inches (48 cm) wide and 14 cm (35.5 cm) high.

Woven Place Mats

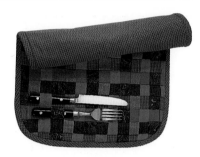

Materials

For each mat:

- Assorted fabric scraps to make 19 strips, each 15 inches (38 cm) long by 1⅞ inches (4.8 cm) wide; and 14 strips, 20 inches (50.5 cm) long by 1⅞ inches (4.8 cm) wide

- For the back, one piece of fabric 19 inches by 14 inches (48 cm by 35.5 cm)

- For binding, approximately 63 inches (160 cm) extra-wide double-fold bias binding, or a bias strip of fabric this length and 1⅞ inches (4.8 cm) wide

- For ties, a 30-inch (76-cm) length of bias as above

- Fusible fleece, 19 inches by 14 inches (48 cm by 35.5 cm)

Optional but very useful:

- Bias tape maker, 25 mm
- Small diameter tube turner
- Rotary cutter and mat

Instructions

Although the bias tape maker (shown on page 53) is listed as an optional tool, it enables you to press long edges of fabric strips in a fraction of the time it would take otherwise. As you pull a strip through the tape maker, it folds both edges neatly and evenly so you can follow along with the iron to press them in place. To give the mat stability, the fabric strips should be cut on the fabric straight grain rather than on the bias, but the tool works just as well.

❶ Cut fabric strips as described above. For quick results, use a rotary cutter and mat with a see-through ruler.

❷ Fold and press the long edges of the fabric strips to a finished width of 1 inch (2.5 cm).

❸ Place the fusible fleece, glue side up, on the ironing board. Starting at the left edge, arrange the 15-inch (38-cm) strips vertically on the fleece, right side up, with the folded edges abutting. Don't fuse them in place yet.

❹ Weave the 20-inch (50.5-cm) strips through the vertical strips in an over-under pattern, alternating the weaving sequence. Snug each strip up against the preceding one so the fleece isn't visible between them. Fuse the strips to the fleece according to the manufacturer's instructions.

❺ Place the wrong side of the mat back fabric against the exposed side of the fleece. Using a small plate or bowl as a template, mark the corners of the mat to round them slightly. Machine baste 1/4 inch (.5 cm) from the edges, following the marks at the corners.

❻ Fold each of the tie strips in half lengthwise, right sides together, and stitch the long edges with a 1/4-inch (.5-cm) seam. Turn right side out with the tube turner, and press.

❼ Fold the ties in half. Position the ties on one short side of the place mat back, approximately 3 inches (7.5 cm) from the upper and lower edges, with the folds at the mat edge and the ends toward the center of the mat. Baste on the original basting stitching line.

❽ Apply bias binding around the edges as described on page 53.

Bias Strips and Bindings

You can easily make your own bias bindings and bias strips for weaving with a bias tape maker, available in a range of sizes at fabric stores and from mail order notions suppliers. The tape maker is just as handy for pressing under the long edges of fabric strips cut on the straight grain, as shown in the photo opposite.

For the smoothest finished bindings, cut fabric strips on the true fabric bias—at a 45-degree angle to the selvage. Cut the strips to the width needed for the tape maker you are using. Use a rotary cutter and see-through ruler to cut quickly and accurately.

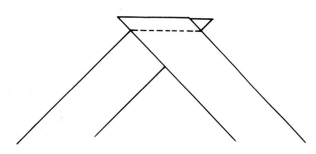

To join bias strips, stitch them with right sides together along the straight grain of the fabric as shown.

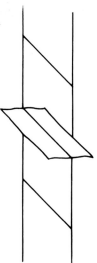

CONTINUOUS BIAS

When you need considerable yardage, it is easier to join the fabric ends before cutting the bias strips.

1 Fold a rectangular piece of fabric along the true bias, beginning at a lower corner. Cut along the foldline.

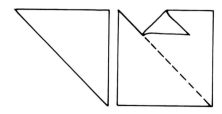

2 Sew the small triangle to the other edge of the fabric, matching the lengthwise grainlines. Press the seam open.

3 Beginning at one bias-cut end, mark off the bias strip widths.

4 With right sides together, pin the two crossgrain ends together to form a tube, offsetting edges so that one strip width extends beyond each end as shown.

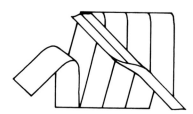

5 Cut along the marked lines to make a continuous bias strip.

4 On the right side, press the tape toward the edge of the piece, taking care not to erase the creases in the tape.

5 Fold the tape over the edge of the piece so that the folded edge covers the first stitching line. Glue baste, if desired. Stitch from the right side in the ditch formed by the previous seamline, making sure to catch the folded edge of the tape on the reverse side.

APPLYING A BIAS BINDING

1 If you are using self bias, fold and press the bias fabric strip with the tape maker as directed. Then fold the piece lengthwise, not quite in half, so that one side extends slightly beyond the other. With purchased double-fold bias tape, re-press the center fold as above if the tape doesn't come this way.

2 Place the piece to be bound with its right side up. side down, aligning the edges. Stitch along the crease of the tape nearest the edge. The seam width will depend upon the tape width.

3 When binding the outer edge of a piece, fold under approximately ½ inch (1 cm) at the end of the tape to overlap the beginning.

With a bias tape maker, both long edges of a fabric strip can be turned under and pressed at the same time.

Baby's Birthday Pillow

Petals fold inward and button in place to make a bud, then open up to reveal the child's own portrait at the flower's center—with a lucky ladybug looking on. A young child will have hours of fun with his personalized peekaboo game, and in later years will have a very special heirloom to treasure.

A custom photo shop or copy shop can produce a full-color iron-on transfer from your photo or slide. Some will also transfer the image to your fabric, or you might find a custom T-shirt shop that will provide this service. You can also do this step at home. Ask for instructions when you have the transfer made and follow them carefully. If you choose a textured or heat-sensitive fabric for the pillow as we did, have the photo reproduced on a separate piece of plain cotton broadcloth.

The pillow cover is made of nubby silk in assorted pale colors, with silver lamé for the trellis pattern behind the flower. Each petal is a double layer of fabric, a different color front and back. A shirred strip edges the pillow. The finished size is 14 by 17 inches (35.5 by 43 cm).

DESIGNED BY MAGGIE ROTMAN

DESIGNED BY
MAGGIE ROTMAN

Materials

- Photo, transferred onto fabric

- Silk or other fabric to make up the front and back of the pillow cover, and for the shirred welt around the perimeter

- Smaller fabric scraps for flower petals and stem

- Silver fabric, if desired, for the trellis design

- Pillow form, 14 by 17 inches (35.5 by 43 cm), or inner pillow (see Options)

- Small ladybug charm or button

- Zipper, 12 inches (30.5 cm)

Instructions

1 Enlarge and trace the flower petal and stem patterns onto stiff paper or light cardboard and cut them out.

2 For the pillow front, assemble scraps to make a piece 15 by 18 inches (38 by 45.3 cm). Measurements allow for ½-inch (1.3-cm) seams.

3 For the back, cut or assemble two pieces each 15 by 9½ inches (38 by 24 cm).

4 To install the zipper, pin with right sides together along one 15-inch (38-cm) side. Stitch in 1½ inches (3.8 cm) from each end and baste the remainder of the seam. Press open. Center the open zipper over the basted portion of the seam. Baste and stitch one side of the zipper to the seam allowance, keeping the teeth even with the seamline. Close the zipper and stitch both sides from the right side.

5 To make the flower petals, first trim the photo image as desired and measure the perimeter. Determine the number of petals needed to surround the image. For the pillow illustrated, the photo is 3½ by 4½ inches (9 cm by 11.5 cm), and 16 petals of each size were used.

Layer the petal fabrics, wrong sides together, and trace around the pattern for the desired number of each petal. Work machine satin stitch around the curved outer edges of each through both thicknesses. Trim the petals close to the stitching and across the bases.

6 Cut out the flower stem. Position the photo image and the stem on the pillow front. Work satin stitch around the stem.

7 Arrange the petals around the photo image in two layers, larger ones first. Place them so that the bases of the petals create a smooth line around the photo. Machine baste in place, stitching close to the petal bases, then work satin stitch over the basting.

8 Sew a button to the underside of one of the large petals at one side of the photo, and work a button loop on the underside of a petal directly opposite. Stitch the ladybug securely onto the upper side of a small petal.

9 For the shirred welt, piece fabrics to make a strip 3 inches (7.5 cm) wide and 62 inches (157 cm) long, or twice the perimeter measurement of the pillow form. Work gathering stitch along each long edge of the strip, ½ inch (1.3 cm) from the edge.

10 Gather up the strip to fit the cover. It is easiest to gather both sides at the same time. Stitch one edge of the strip to one cover section with right sides together and ½ inch (1.3 cm) seam allowance. Stitch the other cover section the same way. Trim corners as necessary, and turn through the zipper opening to insert the pillow form.

Options

Instead of using a purchased pillow form, you might make an inner pillow of muslin and stuff it with fiberfill. Cut two pieces of muslin the same size as the pillow front. Cut a strip for the pillow edge, 3 inches (7.5 cm) wide and 63 inches (160 cm) long. Join the ends of the strip and sew it to one of the larger pieces. Attach the other large piece, leaving an opening for turning and filling.

Baby's Birthday Pillow appliqués

Seam allowance not included—see instructions
Patterns are 50% of actual size

PETALS   STEM

Tooth Bear-er

DESIGNED BY BETH HILL

Velveteen patchwork makes an appropriately elegant coat for the bear whose job it is to deliver a tooth to the Tooth Fairy. The heart-shaped pocket (this one was made of a scrap from mom's wedding dress) provides safekeeping for the tooth—and the subsequent reward. For an older child or a deserving adult, he can serve as bear-er of a very special gift, a piece of jewelry, or an antique hankie.

This bear is approximately 17 inches (43 cm) from head to toe.

Materials

- Fabric scraps to make up the pattern pieces
- Small black scrap for nose
- Lightweight cotton muslin, enough for pattern pieces
- Fiberfill for stuffing
- Eyes: safety-lock eyes, or buttons
- Dollmaker's needle or long darning needle
- Decorative thread for topstitching patchwork, if desired
- Neck ribbon

Instructions

Seam allowance of ¼ inch (.7 cm) is included on pattern pieces. Sew all seams with fabrics right side together unless instructed otherwise.

❶ Enlarge the pattern and cut the pieces from paper. The pattern can be reduced or enlarged for a smaller or larger bear; remember to adjust the seam allowances accordingly.Cut the pieces from muslin if you plan to piece (or cut each from a solid piece of fabric). Cut four ears (use different fabrics for inner and outer sections if you like). Cut two heart-shaped pieces, and a third from the lace if desired. Assemble scraps for piecing the body, arms, legs, and head.

❷ To make the patchwork sections, refer to the detailed instructions on page 73. If desired, embellish along patchwork seamlines with decorative thread and machine embroidery stitches.

❸ Sew the front sections together along the center front. Sew the back sections along the center back, leaving open as marked.

❹ Sew ear sections together around the curved edges. Clip seam allowances and turn right side out. Make a tuck approximately ¼ inch (1 cm) wide with both fabric layers at the unfinished edge. Baste the raw edges together. Baste to the head front, inner side of ear to right side of fabric, with raw edges aligned.

❺ Baste lace to the right side of one heart. Stitch heart sections with a scant ¼-inch (.5 cm) seam allowance, leaving an opening for turning. Clip seam allowances and turn right side out. Stitch the opening. Stitch to the body left front by hand or machine, leaving the upper edges free.

❻ Stitch the arm sections, leaving open across the tops. Clip and turn. Stuff lightly and baste across the openings. Baste to the front at the marked positions, paws toward center front.

❼ Stitch leg sections together around all edges, leaving an opening as marked. Clip seam allowances and turn. Match up the front and back seams and baste the legs to the body front with the raw edges aligned and the toes toward the body.

❽ Baste and stitch the body front to the back. Clip curves around the head and turn through the opening in the body back. If safety-lock eyes will be used, attach them before stuffing the bear.

❾ Stuff the legs and close the openings. Stuff head and body and close the back seam.

❿ For the nose, cut a circle of fabric approximately 1½ inches (4 cm) in diameter. Stitch by hand ¼ inch (.7 cm) from the edge to gather the circle. Stuff with a small piece of fiberfill. Stitch in place. Sew on the eyes, stitching them together through the head. Add the neck bow.

Options

Nose and eyes—and a mouth too, if you wish—may be embroidered if the bear is for a small child. It is easiest to do this after stuffing the bear and before closing back seam.

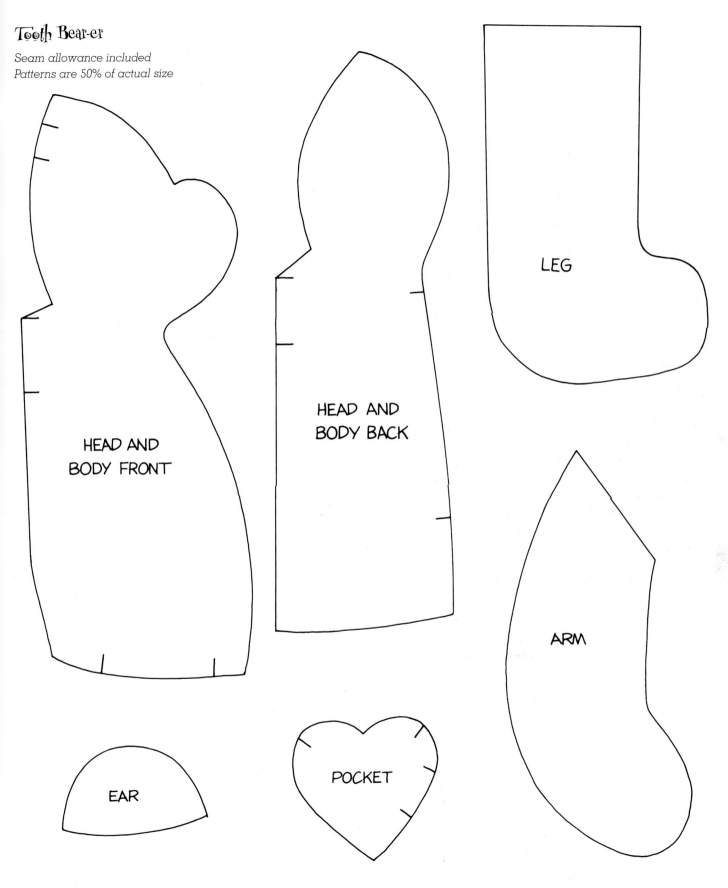

Tooth Bear-er

Seam allowance included
Patterns are 50% of actual size

LEG

HEAD AND
BODY FRONT

HEAD AND
BODY BACK

ARM

EAR

POCKET

Christmas Boot

- Outer fabric
- Lining fabric
- Garment-weight batting
- 8 grommets
- Grommet tool
- Decorative cord for lacing, 1½ yds (1.4 m)

Instructions

Pattern pieces include ¼ inch (.7 cm) seam allowance.

1 Enlarge the pattern and cut from paper. Cut outer boot and lining. Cut batting to the marked front foldline. Trim away seam allowances if fusible batting is used. Cut a strip for the hanging loop 1½ inches wide by 2½ inches long (4 cm by 6.5 cm).

2 Fuse batting to lining sections following the manufacturer's instructions. For sew-in, baste with a narrow zigzag stitch just outside the seamline in the seam allowance. Trim to the stitching.

3 Stitch outer boot sections together around sides and lower edge. Clip the curves, and clip to the seamline at the marked point on the front foldline. Stitch lining sections the same, leaving an opening at the bottom of the foot for turning.

4 Fold the loop strip in half, lengthwise, right side out. Press. Fold in both long edges to the center crease; press. Stitch close to both long edges.

5 Pin the loop at the back seamline of the outer boot, on the right side, with the ends aligned with the upper edge of the boot.

6 With the outer boot right side out and the lining wrong side out, insert the outer boot into the lining and pin upper edges together. Stitch. Turn right side out through the lining opening. Press, and topstitch around upper edge if desired.

An expandable boot holds more goodies than a mere stocking. We've chosen bright holiday-red corduroy for ours, and lined it with colorful checked cotton.

The pattern allows for all sorts of decoration. Add some fancy braid, or a monogram, or appliqué. You might make it in patchwork and incorporate several Christmastime prints.

7 On the outside, crease each front section along the marked foldline. Topstitch approximately ¼ inch (.5 cm) from the edge, stitching as far toward the foot as possible.

8 Attach four grommets along each front edge, and lace up the boot.

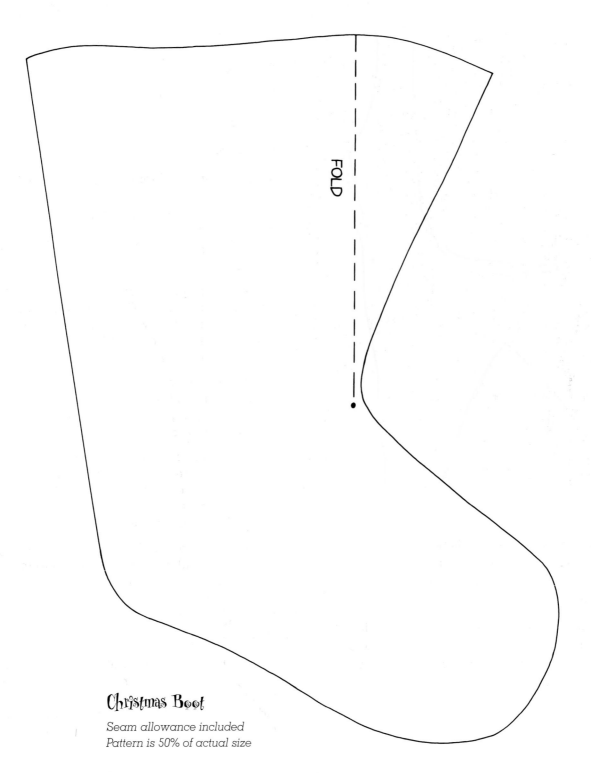

FOLD

Christmas Boot

Seam allowance included
Pattern is 50% of actual size

Christmas Tree Skirt

DESIGNED BY JOYCE BALDWIN

An old white sheet under the Christmas tree serves perfectly well, but can look a bit forlorn once the pretty packages are opened and gone. A specially designed tree skirt provides the festive backdrop your carefully decorated tree deserves.

This designer collects sheep ornaments of every description and continues the theme on the tree skirt with fuzzy sheep appliqués cut from synthetic fleece, dressed up for the season with red and green neck bows and tiny bells. Sprigs of holly feature red bead berries, and white yarn for the tie quilting simulates a light snowfall.

We have perhaps expanded a bit on the definition of "scrap" by using a whole piece of cloth for the background. For the second skirt that you make to give away, it might be fun to piece a background of colorful Christmas prints.

The finished skirt is approximately 46 inches (118 cm) in diameter.

Materials

- For the upper skirt layer, 1⅜ yds (1.3 m) red dotted fabric, 45 inches (115 cm) wide

- For the skirt lining, 1⅜ yds (1.3 m) inexpensive cotton, such as muslin, or a square cut from that old sheet

- Quilt batting, a 45-inch (115-cm) square

- Paper-backed fusible web, ½ yard (.5 m)

- Prefinished ruffle 1½ inches (4 cm) wide, 4 yards (3.7 m)

- Bias-cut fabric strip 1⅞ inch (4.8 cm) wide and 54 inches (137 cm) long, pieced from scraps of fabric from the upper skirt, or purchased double-fold bias tape

- Scraps of white synthetic fur for the sheep

- Scraps of black cotton for the sheep's faces and feet

- For the neck bow for each sheep, ½ yd (.5 m) double-faced red or green satin ribbon ⅛ inch (.3 cm) wide

- One ear for each sheep: 1½ inches (3.5 cm) double-faced black satin ribbon ¼ inch (.7 cm) wide

- For the eyes, ¼-inch (.7-cm) two-hole white pearl buttons, one for each sheep

- One small bell for each sheep

- Scraps of green calico for holly leaves

- Approximately 36 small red beads for berries

- White yarn for tie quilting

Optional, but handy:

- 25 mm bias tape maker

Instructions

❶ Trace pattern pieces for the motifs and cut out of paper. From fabrics, cut sheep bodies and features, and holly leaves (three for each sprig).

❷ Trim a 45-inch (115-cm) square from the skirt and lining fabrics and the batting. Fold each piece in half, then in half the other way, and mark the center. Draw the largest possible circle on each piece using a pencil-and-string compass. Cut the circles.

❸ At the center of each piece, mark and cut out a circle approximately 8 inches (20 cm) in diameter, or as needed to fit your tree and stand. Make a slash from the outer edge to the inner edge of each piece.

❹ Temporarily position sheep bodies on the upper skirt. Slip feet and faces under the bodies, matching to the dotted lines. Fold ribbons for ears as shown in the illustration and slip ends under the head; pin. Remove the bodies. Fuse the faces and feet to the skirt and zigzag around the edges. Stitch the ears in place. Fuse the bodies in place; zigzag the edges. Sew an "eye" at the marked spot on each face.

❺ Cut two 8-inch (20-cm) lengths of ribbon for each neck bow. Sew one end of each to marked spots under the neck and at the back, turning under the ends. Slip the bell over one ribbon end and tie the bows.

❻ Fuse holly leaves to the skirt in sprigs of three, with space between for the bead "berries." Zigzag the edges and sew a line of straight stitch down the center of each for a vein effect. Sew the beads in place.

❼ Smooth the batting to the wrong side of the skirt top. Pin at 4-inch (10-cm) intervals. Pin and machine baste the ruffle around the outer edge, aligning the raw edge of the ruffle to the outer edge of the circle.

8 Baste the lining to the top, right sides together, around the circular edges. Stitch, using ⅜ inch (1 cm) seam allowance. Clip seam allowance around the inner curve and notch the outer curve. Turn right side out and press. Align the layers at the raw edges. Baste close to each edge.

9 Make bias strips with a bias tape maker, or cut strips of purchased binding to bind edges of the opening. Detailed instructions are on pages 52 and 53. If desired, make two pair of ties with another length of bias or with ribbon, and sew opposite one another along the slash.

10 For the tie quilting, mark positions for the stitches on the skirt top. Thread a large-eyed needle with a short length of yarn. At each marked position, take a stitch down through all the layers and back up in almost the same spot. Tie a square knot and trim the yarn ends.

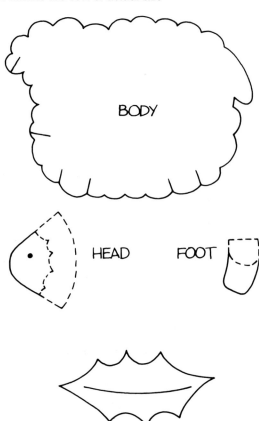

Christmas Skirt appliqués

Patterns are 50% of actual size

BODY

HEAD   FOOT

Baby's Wrap

DESIGNED BY BIRD ROSS

ry this soft, cuddly blanket the next time you need a baby gift that's far from ordinary. It is made with a double layer of cotton flannel, edged with bright cotton squares. All the materials are preshrunk so mom can throw it into the washer and dryer without a worry.

This blanket is 30 by 40 inches (76 by 102 cm) in size. Enlarge it slightly to make a comfortable adult-sized throw for chilly evenings.

Materials

- Fabrics for face and reverse sides of blanket
- Fabric scraps for edging
- Plenty of thread

Instructions

1 For the central part of the blanket, choose baby-soft fabrics, preferably all cotton. Experiment with combinations of patterns and colors to make the two sides different, and try patterned fabrics for the edging squares, too. Preshrink all fabrics thoroughly by machine washing and drying them two or three times.

2 Cut the main fabric pieces slightly larger than the finished size. The squares can be small—perhaps 2 inches (5 cm) for a small print—or 4 to 5 inches (10 to 13 cm) for a large, cartoony print. Cut a few more than you think you will need, and a few for practice if you have never tried this technique.

3 Machine baste the central pieces with wrong sides together, stitching approximately ½ inch (1.5 cm) from the edges.

4 Make the blanket according to the detailed instructions on pages 30 and 31. So that it will be very soft, the blanket is not stitched all over the surface, but is quilted just enough to secure and decorate the edging.

C ombine scraps in wonderful ways for out-of-the-ordinary wearables. It just takes a little imagination and a little spare time.

Accessories From Head To Toe

DESIGNED BY MARY KAY WEST

Cheerful floral prints make summertime accessories that are as refreshing as a walk through a garden. Add this trio to the most basic summer dress to create an eye-catching ensemble.

Shoes

And why not? For a special occasion—or any day that should be special, make a pair of shoes that are just for fun. There is no sewing involved!

Work with fabric-covered shoes. If they have been dyed, test to be sure the dye doesn't run when glue is applied. Choose a non-transparent fabric, fairly light in weight, with a little give. Blouse-weight polyester works well. Test a small piece of fabric with the glue to be sure the glue won't seep through and that the fabric color is unchanged after the glue has

dried. It is a good idea to practice first with non-essential shoes to get a feel for the technique.

Use fabric glue that won't be affected by water after it is dry. Notions suppliers carry this product.

Materials

- Fabric-covered shoes
- Fabric, ¾ yd (.7 m) to cover an average pair of high-heeled shoes
- Fabric glue, the water-resistant type
- Paintbrush
- Table knife or screwdriver
- Craft knife with a sharp new blade

1 Make sure shoes are clean and dry. Have a single piece of fabric large enough to cover the entire shoe.

2 Start at the toe, and with the paintbrush spread glue evenly over an area of about 1 inch (2.5 cm) square. Work with the bias grain of the fabric running the length of the shoe. Start with a corner of fabric and press it smoothly to the glued section. With a table knife or screwdriver, tuck in the fabric firmly between the upper and the sole. Don't trim yet.

3 Continue this way up the toe and around the sides at the toe area. When you reach the point where you can no longer maneuver the fabric, cut carefully along the shoe opening, cutting no closer than ⅝ inch (1.5 cm) from the edge of the shoe.

4 Continue along until the shoe is covered. Tuck in the fabric along the seam at the back of the upper heel. If your shoe heels are not covered with fabric, don't cover them, but tuck in the fabric above the heels as you have been doing.

5 Allow the shoes to dry thoroughly. Trim away the excess fabric around the soles using a very sharp craft knife or razor blade.

6 Trim around the opening to leave a fabric margin of approximately ⅝ inch (1.5 cm). Working with a small section at a time, spread glue along the edge and the upper ½ inch (1.3 cm) or so inside. Turn the fabric to the inside, clipping as necessary so it will fit smoothly.

Options

You might wish to add a folded strip of bias-cut fabric around the top. Trim the fabric along the upper edge. Glue the bias with a folded edge around the outer shoe, then fold the strip to the inside and glue in place.

Floral Pin and Earrings

Here is a jewelry-making technique that almost guarantees success. It is easy to do and it works well with nearly any lighter weight fabric. Add a purchased bar pin, or use the same design for a barrette.

Follow the directions with the fabric stiffener, and always test it first with a sample of your fabric. Any liquid can react unpredictably with the dyes in fabric.

Materials

- Fabric scraps
- Fabric stiffener
- Shiny puff paint (available in crafts supply stores)
- White glue
- Findings: earring backs, bar pin or barrette

Instructions

Pin

1 Cut five fabric circles (better if they aren't quite perfect) with different diameters, ranging from approximately 1½ inches (3.5 cm) to 5 inches (12.5 cm). Cut four or five scallops around each one.

2 Dampen a circle with fabric stiffener and shape it in a flowerlike way. Allow it to dry. Do the same with the other circles.

3 Trim away any frayed threads around the pieces. Apply puff paint around the edges. Allow them to dry.

4 Layer the pieces to form the flower. Use white glue or a few hand stitches to hold the petals together. Add several dots of puff paint for the flower's center.

5 Glue or stitch the pin or barrette to the back.

Earrings

For each earring, cut a fabric circle approximately 1½ inches (4 cm) in diameter, then follow the instructions for the pin, above. Stitch or glue earring backs in place after the flowers have dried completely.

Scarf and Ribbon Earrings

DESIGNED BY
MARY KAY WEST

Materials

For scarf:

- Fabric

For earrings:

- Fabric scraps
- Fabric stiffener
- Shiny puff paint
- Earring backs

Instructions

Scarf

For a long scarf, cut the rectangle on the lengthwise grain of the fabric if possible. Hem with a serger set for a narrow rolled hem. On a sewing machine, use a rolled hem presser foot if you have one.

This technique works well with lightweight fabrics: If your machine's needle position is adjustable, set it to correspond with one of the grooves on the bottom of the manual buttonhole presser foot. Set the zigzag stitch at medium width and short length, and let the groove guide the fabric as you overcast the edge.

Earrings

For each earring, cut a fabric strip approximately 4 inches (10 cm) long and ¾ inch (2 cm) wide. Make the earrings according to the instructions on page 69, but mold each strip into a ribbon-candy shape by folding it back and forth around a knitting needle or large nail.

A pretty new scarf always perks up the wardrobe. With a remnant of blouse fabric and a machine-rolled hem, this one is quick to make. Add matching earrings for an accessory duo that's ready to go this very evening.

Elegant Patchwork Bag

DESIGNED BY
LORI KERR

Velvet, brocade, satin, and taffeta patches are embellished with all kinds of decorative threads and stitches to create a bag that is really very practical. Here is the place to experiment with all the latest ornamental threads and to play with your machine's embroidery stitches. Put together a unique patchwork that features the best of your scrap collection.

Our bag has a lining and upper section of black moire taffeta, and a few antique buttons for accent. It is approximately 6½ inches (17 cm) wide and 15 inches (38 cm) long.

Materials

- Fabric for upper bag/lining
- Scraps for piecing
- Muslin for backing
- Thick cord for strap, approximately 1 yd (1 m)
- Fine cord or ribbon for drawstring, ¾ yd (.7 m)
- Assorted decorative threads
- Assorted heavy threads or yarn for couching
- Seed beads for fringe, and beading needle
- Decorative buttons and beads for ornamentation, as desired

Instructions

Seam allowance of ½ inch (1 cm) is included in cutting dimensions.

Assembly and Embellishment

1 For the backing, cut two muslin pieces 7½ inches (17 cm) wide and 10 inches (25.5 cm) long. For the bag front/lining, cut two pieces 7½ inches (17 cm) wide and 22 inches (55.5 cm) long.

2 Cut one end of each muslin and front/lining piece to form a point at the center. Cut them together for uniformity.

3 For the patchwork, piece small scraps to both muslin sections. Detailed instructions are on page 73.

4 Decorate the patchwork. Use every decorative thread you would like to try. Edge the patches, stitch designs, use the machine's decorative stitches. Couch some heavier thread or yarn: arrange it in a pattern and zigzag over it with invisible or contrasting thread. A cording presser foot guides the couched thread neatly.

5 Work a vertical ½-inch (1.5-cm) buttonhole at the center of one (the front) top/lining section beginning 2¼ inches (5.5 cm) from the short straight edge. Reinforce behind it with a scrap of firm interfacing.

6 Fold the upper straight edge of each top/lining ½ inch (1 cm) to the wrong side. Press. Position this edge over the straight edge of the patchwork, overlapping by the width of the seam allowance. Sew it in place with a decorative stitch and thread, stitching close to the fold.

7 Stitch the two sections with right sides together, leaving an opening along one lining seam for turning. Trim and turn right side out.

8 Push the lining into the bag, smoothing the fabrics together at the lower pointed end of the bag. Press the fold that forms around the top of the bag and stitch close to the fold with a decorative stitch. Close the opening.

Finishing

1 Stitch the casing for the drawstring. Mark parallel lines around the bag at the upper and lower ends of the buttonhole. Stitch around them. Thread cord through the casing.

2 Cut two small pieces of the lining fabric; fold and press under the edges to form two squares approximately 1 inch (2.5 cm) in size.

3 Cut the thick cord to the desired length—approximately 40 inches (1 m) for a shoulder strap or 34 inches (86 cm) if you will carry the bag over your arm. Apply a few drops of fray retardant to the cut ends. Position one end about 1 inch (2.5 cm) below the drawstring casing at the side seamline inside the bag. Arrange one of the small squares over it and baste it in place. From the right side, stitch the cord and patch securely with decorative thread and stitches, if you like. Stitch the other end of the cord to the other side of the bag in the same way.

4 For accent, sew on buttons and beads.

5 Add a beaded fringe along the lower edge seamline if you wish. Thread the beading needle with strong, lightweight thread and take several stitches at one end of the lower edge. String a dozen or so beads. Push the needle through the next to last bead on the thread and back through the strand. Take one or two stitches at the point where you began, then several more to the point where you will work the next strand. Continue along the lower edge this way, perhaps adding a single decorative bead at the center point. Our bag has 44 strands, each approximately 1¼ inches (3 cm) in length.

Piecing Fabrics

Any project in which you are trying to utilize scraps of fabric often requires combining bits of fabric to make up a single piece large enough to fit your needs. Sometimes, too, pieced fabrics simply create a more interesting effect than a single piece of fabric can produce.

Whenever you piece fabrics to fit a pattern, make the patchwork section slightly larger all around than the pattern, then trim it to size after the piecing is finished. The piecing seams, especially when there are many, can draw up the fabric, resulting in a completed piece that is smaller than the pattern.

Treat embroidered patchwork the same way. Work embellishment stitching on the pieced section before trimming it to fit a pattern piece.

Here is a quick and easy way to piece strips or "crazy" patches to fit a pattern.

1 Cut pattern pieces out of lightweight muslin, adding generous seam allowance around the edges.

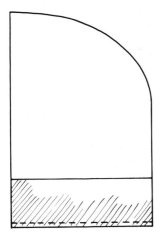

2 Assemble the scraps or strips to be used. Beginning at one edge or lower corner of the muslin piece, position a fabric piece, right side up, with outer edges extending to the edges of the muslin. Stitch the fabric to the muslin along one seam allowance to secure it.

3 Place a second piece face down on the first with the inner edges aligned. Stitch the two pieces together and to the muslin along this edge with ¼ inch (.7 cm) seam allowance.

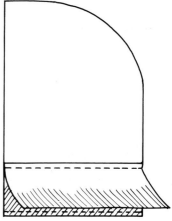

4 Flip the second piece over so the right side is up, and press the seam.

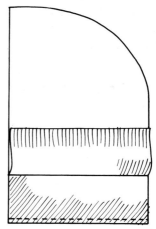

5 If an edge of a patch will remain visible after subsequent pieces are added, press that edge under before sewing the patch in place.

6 Continue this way until the muslin is covered. Baste the patches to the muslin around the seam allowance. Trim excess fabric to the muslin edges.

A Trio of Hats

DESIGNED BY LIZ SPEAR

Hand weavers devote so much time to creating their fabrics that they become true masters at using up every small scrap. Designer Liz Spear combines hers in wonderfully soft, colorful hats, adding other fabrics here and there for variety and texture. Handwoven fabric certainly is not essential—all three hat styles adapt quite readily to any fabric that has a little give to it.

Patchwork Beret

A hat that's always chic and appropriate, this beret features a top of pieced handwoven fabrics. The underside and brim are corduroy, and it's lined with soft lightweight silk.

Materials

- Scraps to piece for the top (or cut it as one piece if desired)
- The same or different fabric for the underside and band.
- Lining fabric

Instructions

Use ⅜ inch (1 cm) seam allowance except when instructed otherwise.

1 Enlarge the pattern and cut pattern pieces from paper in your size. From fabric, cut one underside. For the band, measure your head size and on the fabric crossgrain cut one piece that length plus ¾ inch (2 cm) and 3 inches (7.5 cm) wide. Cut one top if you are not piecing it. Cut lining with the top and underside pattern pieces.

2 To piece the top, stitch rectangular scraps of fabric with right sides together and ¼ inch (.7 cm) seam allowance, pressing after each seam. Make the patchwork piece slightly larger than the top pattern, then trim it to size.

3 Join the ends of the side section, right sides together. Join the ends of the lining side in the same way.

4 Sew the top to the side outer edge, right sides together. Sew the lining top and side the same way.

5 Place the lining inside the hat. Pin, then stitch the edges together around the opening, stitching approximately ¼ inch (1 cm) from the edge.

6 Sew on the band. It is easier to attach it before joining the ends. Start at the seamline at one end of the band, aligning it with the hat seam. Pin the right side of the band to the lining side of the hat, easing as necessary. Stitch, and press seam allowances toward the band. Join the ends of the band.

7 Fold under and press the seam allowance on the other edge of the band. Fold the band to the outside of the hat and pin so that the folded edge of the band just covers the previous stitching line. Stitch close to the edge by hand or machine.

Patchwork Beret

Seam allowance included
Patterns are 25% of actual size

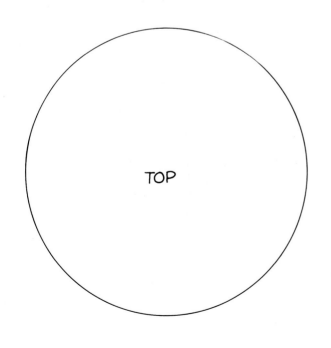

TOP

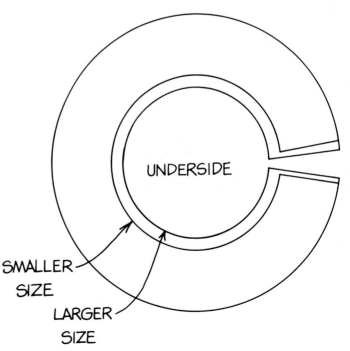

UNDERSIDE

SMALLER SIZE

LARGER SIZE

The Roundtop Hat

A double layer of fabric makes it reversible, and it's thoroughly comfortable in any season. Make it of wool and pull the long sides down over your ears to ward off winter's worst storms. Use lightweight fabrics for the summer version and turn up the edges in a free-spirited way.

Materials

Fabrics: Cut all four pieces from the same fabric, or use a different one for each.

Instructions

All seam allowances are ⅜ inch (1 cm).

1 Enlarge the pattern and cut a paper pattern in your size. Cut two crown sections. For sides, cut two fabric rectangles with the longer measurement on the cross-grain of the fabric: For the smaller hat size, cut both pieces 25 inches (63.5 cm) wide. Cut one piece 9 inches (23 cm) long and the other 7 inches (18 cm) long. For the larger size, cut the rectangles the same length as for the smaller size, but 26 inches (66 cm) wide.

2 Join the short ends of each rectangular piece, with right sides together, to form a tube.

3 Place the two crown sections with their wrong sides together. Pin and stitch one of the tubes to the crowns, right sides together. Position the other tube against the other crown, right sides together, and stitch along the previous stitching line.

4 Turn the hat so the sides are together, the shorter side piece on the outside. On the longer side piece, press the raw edge ½ inch (1 cm) to its wrong side. Fold this edge up over the raw edge of the shorter piece, matching edges. Smooth the fabric and pin. Machine stitch close to the folded edge of the longer section. For loosely woven or stretchy fabrics, use a moderately open zigzag stitch.

DESIGNED BY LIZ SPEAR

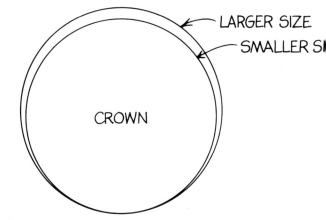

LARGER SIZE

SMALLER S[...]

CROWN

Seam allowance included
Pattern is 25% of actual size

❶ Cut six fabric sections for the crown. Cut one band on the fabric crossgrain: head measurement plus ¾ inch (2 cm) in length, 4 inches (10 cm) wide. Cut lining.

❷ Stitch the crown pieces with right sides together and ¼ inch (.7 cm) seam allowance. Press each seam.

❸ Press creases across the lining to mark it into sixths.

❹ Baste lining to the completed crown with wrong sides together, matching creases to seams in the crown. Make a small tuck at each crease, if necessary, to fit the lining to the crown.

❺ Attach the band. Start and end at the seamlines on the band ends, aligning them with a hat seam. Pin the right side of the band to the lining side of the hat, easing as necessary. Stitch, a ⅜-inch (1-cm) seam. Press seam allowances toward the band. Join the ends of the band.

❻ Fold under and press ⅜ inch (1 cm) seam allowance on the other edge of the band. Fold the band to the outside of the hat and pin so that the folded edge of the band just covers the previous stitching line. Stitch close to the edge by hand or machine.

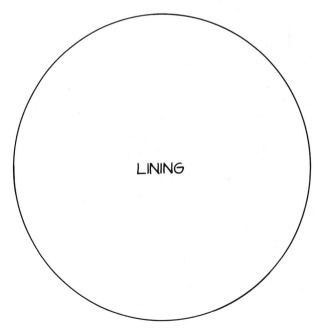

LINING

Seam sllowance included
Patterns are 25% of actual size

DESIGNED BY LIZ SPEAR

Sporty Beanie

It's an excellent candidate for scrap piecing because of its compound construction. You can work in more fabrics still if you divide each crown section in half (be sure to add a narrow seam allowance at each cut edge). The band can be pieced, too, but cut the sections with the fabric crossgrain going around the head. Most fabrics stretch slightly in this direction.

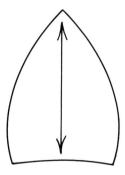

CROWN SECTION

Materials

■ Fabric, for hat and band
■ Lining

Beaded Patchwork Bag

DESIGNED BY PAT TAYLOR

On the outside it's a cheerful patchwork of brilliantly colored silk noil scraps, inside is a bright cotton print, and colorful wooden beads provide accents here and there. The bag is fun to put together and fun to carry. The design is so adaptable you might want to make another of synthetic suede to use with suits, and yet another in rich brocade to accompany the basic black evening dress.

Materials

- Fabric for outer bag and lining cut to pattern size, or, for the outer bag, lightweight muslin and scraps to piece

- Decorative cord for strap, approximately 1¼ yds (1.15 m.). We used three strands of rattail cord knotted together

- Beads to embellish the strap, if desired

- Button or large bead for front fastener

Instructions

1 Enlarge the pattern and cut paper pattern piece.

2 Cut one piece of outer fabric and one lining for the bag back/flap. Then fold the pattern along the dotted line and cut another of each for the bag front. For a pieced bag, cut the outer bag pieces from muslin and refer to the instructions on page 73 for piecing.

3 Cut a piece of cord for the button loop, using the button as a guide for measuring. Baste it to the seam allowance of the flap point, ends aligned with the fabric edge.

4 With right sides together, stitch each outer section to its lining with a very narrow (³⁄₁₆ inch or .5 cm) seam allowance. Leave an opening at the lower edge for turning. Turn, press, and stitch across the openings.

5 With right sides together, stitch the bag front to the back along the sides and lower edge with a narrow seam allowance.

6 If you are adding beads, string them onto the cord. Make two knots close together near each end of the cord. By hand, stitch the cord just inside the upper edge of the bag at each side seam, stitching between the knots. Sew the button to the bag front.

Options

As an alternative, use a continuous length of bias tape to form the bag strap and bind the edges. Use approximately 1½ yds (1.4 m) ½-inch (1.3-cm) double-fold tape, or make your own with a fabric strip and bias tape maker. Detailed instructions for making and applying bias binding are on page 52 and 53.

Beaded Patchwork Bag

Seam allowance included
Pattern is 50% of actual size

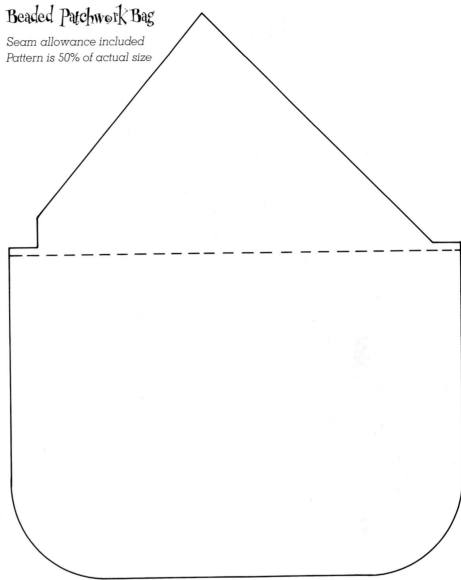

Make the bag according to the instructions above through step 3. On the bag front, stitch outer fabric to lining with right sides together only across the upper edge. On the back section, stitch just the outer edges of the flap. Then place the bag front and back with lining sides together. Stitch around the sides and lower edge and trim away most of the seam allowance. Bind the edges with the tape, beginning at an upper edge of the bag. At the opposite upper edge, continue stitching along the folded edges of the binding.

Shaped Belt

DESIGNED BY MARY PARKER

ather in the waistline of a tunic with a belt of the same fabric. This one features a pattern of waves in harmonizing colors. For accent, add a few polymer buttons decorated with brightly colored fish in the same colors.

Materials

- Background fabric, ¼ yard (.25 m) for outer belt and lining

- Scraps for trim in assorted colors, pieced to make three bias strips each ⅞ inch (2.3 cm) wide and 40 inches (101 cm) long. (For more about bias strips, see page 52.)

  - Fusible fleece, ⅛ yard (.15 m)

  - 3-inch (7.5-cm) strip of heavy-duty hook and loop tape, 1½ inches (3.8 cm) wide

  - Decorative beads or buttons

  Optional but very helpful:

  - 12 mm bias tape maker

1 Make a paper pattern for your belt, using the diagram as a guide. The pattern will include ¼ inch (.7 cm) seam allowance. The pattern piece should be approximately 4½ inches (11.5 cm) longer than your waist measurement, measured over the garments you will wear beneath the belt. It is 3¾ inches (10 cm) wide at center front, tapering to 2½ inches (6.5 cm) for the straight sections. Make the wider front panel approximately one-third to one-half of your waist measurement. Fold the paper in half and use the fold as center front when you draw the pattern so both sides will be the same.

2 Cut two pieces of fabric and one piece of fleece with the pattern. Trim ¼ inch (.7 cm) from all edges of the fleece.

3 Place the fleece on the wrong side of one belt section so that there is a ¼-inch (.7-cm) fabric margin around all edges of the fleece. Fuse according to the manufacturer's instructions.

4 Press under the long edges of the bias strips using the bias tape maker. Alternatively, press the edges ³⁄₁₆ inch (.5 cm) to the wrong side.

5 Arrange the bias strips, right sides up, on the belt to create a design that pleases you. At the back, end the design short of the overlapping area of the belt. Try to hide piecing seams under other strips. With chalk or pins, mark the placement of the two uppermost strips, then remove. Pin the bottom one to the belt, turning under the ends.

6 Sew the pinned strip to the belt, stitching very close to both edges and across the ends. Pin and stitch the remaining strips the same way.

7 Pin the two belt sections with right sides together. Stitch both long edges and one end, using ⅜ inch (1 cm) seam allowance. Turn right side out; press. Press seam allowances at the open end to the inside and stitch the opening close to the edge.

8 Try on the belt and mark the positions of the hook and loop tape sections. Stitch them in place around all edges. Sew on the decorative beads or buttons.

Baggy Ball Cap

DESIGNED BY PAT TAYLOR

Here is a hat to convey your attitude of the moment. Stitch it up in colorful cottons for playful days, or use wool scraps in earthy colors for a more subdued version. The hat's crown is made up of eight segments, each in turn pieced together from whatever combination of scraps you care to assemble.

Materials

- Scraps for patchwork
- Muslin, for patchwork backing
- Lining fabric
- Buckram, for bill
- Button to cover
- Elastic, 3/4 inch (2 cm) wide, cut to head measurement plus 1 inch (2.5 cm)

Instructions

1 Enlarge the pattern and cut pieces from paper. From muslin, cut eight crown sections. From fabric, cut two bill sections. Cut one bill from buckram. Cut eight crown sections from lining.

2 Piece scraps to each muslin crown section. Detailed instructions are on page 73.

3 For the crown, stitch patchwork sections with right sides together and ⅜ inch (1 cm) seam allowance. Join lining sections in the same way.

4 Trim seam allowance from bill interfacing and glue-baste to wrong side of one bill section. Stitch to the other bill section around the sides and front with right sides together and ¼ inch (.7 cm) seam allowance. Clip the seam allowance around the curve; turn and press.

5 Place the lining in the hat, wrong sides together, and pin. Pin the bill to the right side of the hat with raw edges aligned. Stitch and overcast the edges together all the way around.

6 Starting at center back, place one long edge of the elastic to overlap the hat edge by ¼ inch (.7 cm) and to cover the stitching. Pin in quarters, stretching elastic to fit the hat edge, but not stretching the area along the brim. Overlap the ends by 1 inch (2.5 cm). Stitch, using a very narrow zigzag stitch. If your fabric permits, use a ballpoint needle for this step to prevent weakening the elastic.

Baggy Ball Cap

Seam allowance included
Pattern is 50% of actual size

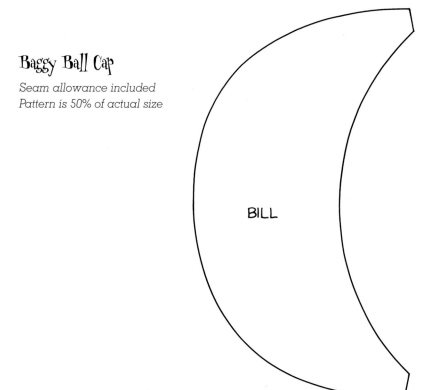

BILL

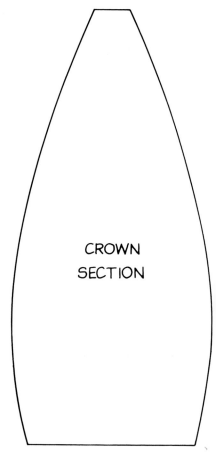

CROWN SECTION

Lacy Bag

DESIGNED BY LORI KERR

This small, elegant bag instantly gives special-occasion status to the most basic outfit. The design is simple, but the intricate lace fabric and unusual embellishments make it seem very elaborate.

The bag is lined in a slightly darker shade to highlight the pattern of the lace. A pearl button, crystal beads, and tassels add shimmer and movement.

Materials

- Lace scraps
- *For lining*, taffeta or similar fabric
- 1 yard (.9 m) decorative braid, ¾ inch (2 cm) wide
- Rayon cord, ¼ inch (.7 cm) diameter, 1 yard (1 m), or desired finished length plus 3 inches (8 cm)

Lacy Bag *(continued from previous page)*

- Adhesive-backed hook and loop tape button

- Glue stick or liquid basting medium

For embellishment:

- Lace motif and button or other ornament for flap front

- Approximately 60 silver-lined crystal seed beads

- Small tassel

Instructions

❶ From lace, cut one bag front and one bag back/flap. Cut the same pieces from lining fabric.

❷ With right sides together, stitch bag front to lining front along the upper straight edge, using ¼ inch (.7 cm) seam allowance. Turn right side out and press.

❸ Place back/flap pieces with wrong sides together, aligning all edges. Position the lined front on top of it, lace side up, and align sides and lower edges with the back piece. With a medium zigzag stitch and working close to the edges, stitch the front to the back along the sides and lower edge. Continue stitching around the flap to secure the lace to the lining.

❹ Position the braid, beginning at the flap, just above the point where front and back join. Fold the braid almost in half, working first with the wider side of the braid and the lining side of the flap. Glue-baste the braid all the way around the edge of the flap and the bag.

❺ Overlap slightly where the end meets the beginning. Fold under the end if the braid is not too thick, or apply a drop of fray retardant to prevent raveling.

❻ Knot the rayon cord 1 inch (2.5 cm) from each end. Tuck the ends into the bag at the flap fold and stitch securely in place.

❼ Press the hook and loop tape button to the underside of the flap and at the corresponding point on the outer front of the bag. Stitch the decorative button on the outer flap. Sew the tassel at the point on the bag's lower edge.

Crewel Vest

This designer created a unique vest from the fragments of an exquisite 18th-century English bed curtain that had been badly burned. The curtain was a tightly woven linen twill fabric embroidered by hand with fine, subtly colored wool yarn. It would have been a crime to cut the piece if it had been in good condition, but in this case the small remaining pieces have been salvaged and used in a way that showcases the magnificent handwork.

The vest was cut from a simple commercial pattern without darts. It deserved a silk lining, and scraps from a daughter's wedding dress were tea-dyed to produce a color more complementary to the linen.

Because the fabric is so fragile, the designer chose not to topstitch around the outer edges of the vest as a means of preventing the lining from rolling to the outside. Instead, she worked feather stitch around the edges on the lining side, catching the lining to the seam allowance of the antique fabric. For the hand stitching she used a double strand of embroidery floss in a color to match the silk.

Recycling wonderful fabrics is always rewarding. To plan the placement of the fabric's design elements, first trace the *seamlines* of your main garment pattern pieces onto transparent paper. Move the traced pieces around on the fabric to determine best pattern placement for cutting.

DESIGNED BY GAY SYMMES

85

Reversible Crusher Hat

The popular crusher hat adapts well to a patchwork design. This one is solid-colored fabric on the reverse side, trimmed with a bias-cut band in a contrasting color. For extra fun with this project, dye or paint plain cotton muslin to get colors and patterns that aren't in your scrap box.

DESIGNED BY PAT TAYLOR

Materials

- Fabric scraps, for outer hat

- Muslin, for patchwork backing

- Fabric for lining

- Lightweight interfacing, if desired, for brim

Optional but helpful:

- 25 mm bias tape maker

Instructions

Seam allowance is included on all pattern pieces.

❶ Enlarge the pattern and cut from paper. Cut the crown, side, and brim from muslin and from lining. Cut a bias strip 24 inches (61 cm) long and 1½ inches (4 cm) wide. If you are using a tape maker, cut to the width instructed. If outer fabric and/or lining are very lightweight, cut interfacing for the brim.

❷ Piece scraps to the muslin for the crown, side, and brim as described on page 73.

3 Fuse or baste interfacing to the wrong side of the brim, if necessary.

4 Stitch together the ends of the patchwork brim and of the lining brim, right sides together, with ⅝ inch (1.5 cm) seam allowance.

5 Stitch the brim sections, right sides together, around the outer edge with ¼ inch (.5 cm) seam allowance. Clip the seam allowance at intervals, turn, and press. Baste the inner edges together, stitching close to the edge. Topstitch the brim, stitching ¼ inch (.5 cm) from the edge and then stitching parallel lines approximately ⅝ inch (1.5 cm) apart.

6 Stitch the short ends of the patchwork side piece with right sides together and ⅝ inch (1.5 cm) seam allowance. Stitch the lining side piece in the same way. Press seams open. Stitch each side to the corresponding crown section with right sides together and ⅝ inch (1.5 cm) seam allowance.

7 Press under the long edges of the bias strip with the tape maker, or ¼ inch (.7 cm).

8 Unfold one edge of the bias strip. Pin the brim to the hat, patchwork sides together, and with the bias strip right side down against the brim lining side, all raw edges aligned. Turn under the overlapping end of the bias strip. Stitch. Press seam allowances toward the crown.

9 Turn the bias strip toward the crown; press, and stitch the remaining folded edge to the lining by hand.

Reversible Crusher Hat

Seam allowance included
Pattern is 50% of actual size

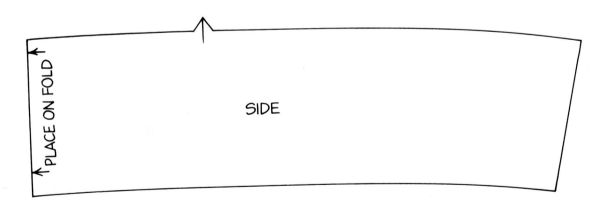

PLACE ON FOLD

SIDE

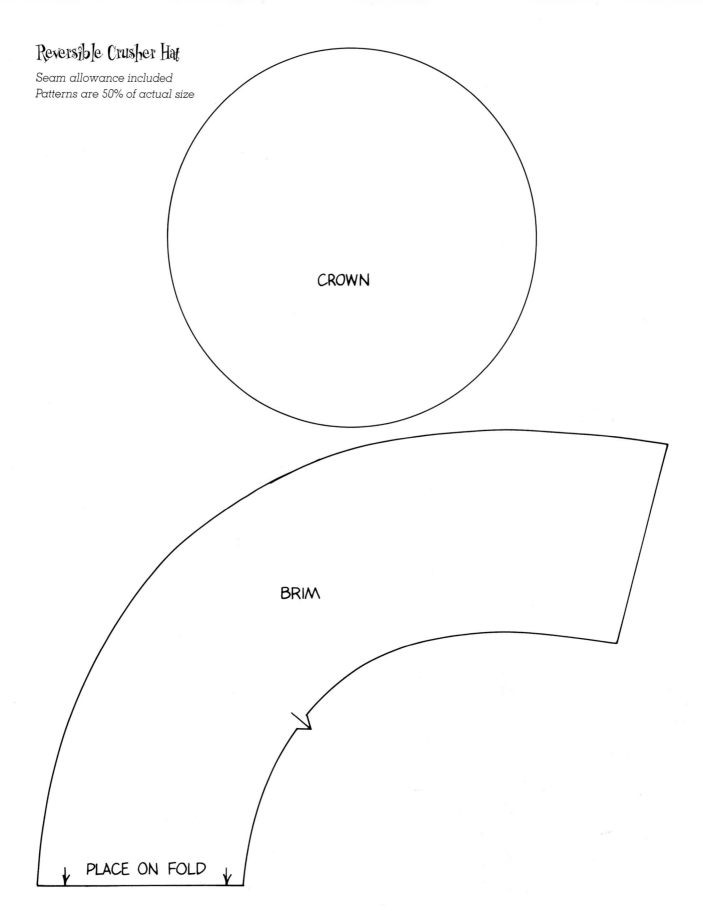

Reversible Crusher Hat

Seam allowance included
Patterns are 50% of actual size

CROWN

BRIM

PLACE ON FOLD

A gift made by hand expresses your thoughtfulness in an especially nice way. Here are suggestions for gifts that let you add your own unique embellishments, and that are quick to make besides.

Cloth Bowls

DESIGNED BY PAT TAYLOR

They're not for soup or cereal, but you'll find no shortage of uses for these decorative fabric bowls. For a clever gift, fill one with toasted pistachio nuts or small scented soaps.

It's great fun to experiment with a variety of fabrics and threads to see what will result. Light to medium weight cotton and silk are the best fabric choices; synthetics won't mold into shape as you sew. Use invisible thread to emphasize fabric patterns and textures. Try contrasting thread in a variety of colors to highlight the stitching—and to get rid of all those spools of thread with just a few yards left.

As a variation, make the bowl of prewashed all-cotton muslin, then paint a picture or design with acrylic paints or fabric marking pens.

Materials

- Fabric scraps. For a bowl approximately 6 inches (15 cm) in diameter and 1½ inches (4 cm) deep you will need approximately ¼ yd (.25 m).

- Thread

- Polyurethane, if desired, for finishing

Instructions

For success with this technique, use a machine with 5 mm stitch width capability. A free arm is also helpful.

1 Cut or tear fabric into strips 1 to 1¼ inches (2.5 to 3 cm) wide. For the bowl base, start with a strip approximately 45 inches (115 cm) long.

2 Set the machine for a zigzag stitch at a moderately long stitch length and at maximum width.

3 For the base, start at one end of the long strip and fold several inches of it in half and in half again so that the piece is approximately ¼ inch (.8 cm) wide. Fold the tube about 1½ to 2 inches (3 to 4 cm) from the end to create a flattened candy cane shape and begin stitching the two sections together at the fold.

4 Coil the folded strip around, abutting the edges and stitching it to the previous round. Twist the folded strip into a tube as you go (the action of the presser foot will help). Twist toward the right to prevent the strip catching in the presser foot. Form a flat oval shape, like a miniature braided rug, for the bottom of the bowl.

5 To attach a new fabric strip, overlap the end approximately ¼ inch (1 cm), then stitch and backstitch to secure it.

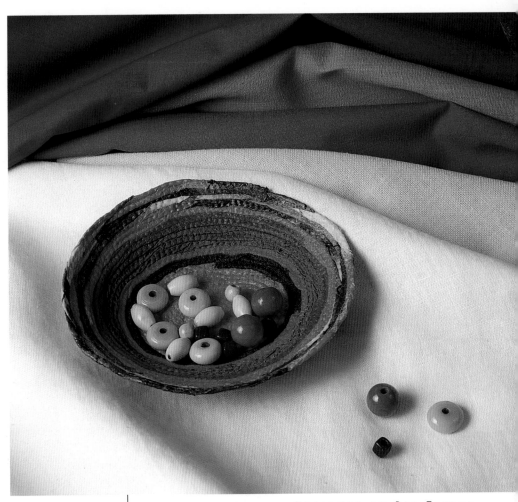

DESIGNED BY PAT TAYLOR

6 Shape the sides of the bowl. Begin to overlap the edges of the strips slightly and evenly. Work over the free arm of the machine, treating the upper side of the work as the outside of the bowl. With a little practice, you'll find that the vessel will almost shape itself.

7 When the upper edge of the bowl is finished, stitch the end of the strip securely in place.

8 Stitch randomly over the finished bowl to stabilize the shape and to join any gaps between strips that you may have missed in the first round of stitching.

9 If desired, coat the finished bowl with polyurethane for added stiffness and soil resistance.

Tailored Tote

DESIGNED BY TERRY TAYLOR

Present your hostess with a six-pack from the latest microbrewery or soft drinks for the patio party in a stylish reusable carrier. Choose a sturdy fabric remnant to support the weight and decorate it with anything you have at hand. We added patches of color with acrylic paint, then used metallic thread to stitch on a few copper stars and glass beads. As an alternative, try a few embroidery stitches over brightly colored appliqué. It's a quick project that makes a great impression!

Materials

- Fabric piece, 10 by 21 inches (25.5 by 53 cm), for the carrier

- Two fabric pieces, 3½ by 14 inches (9 by 35.5 cm), for the handles

- Scraps, beads, buttons, and metallic thread for embellishment

- Wooden dowel, ¾ inch (2 cm) in diameter and 10 inches (25.5 cm) long

Instructions

❶ On the large piece of fabric, press ½ inch (1.3 cm) to the wrong side on all edges, mitering the corners. Stitch the hems with a zigzag stitch, enclosing the raw edges at the same time.

❷ Finish the long edges of the handles the same way.

❸ Add your choice of embellishments to the carrier and handles. Remember the center 5 inches (12.5 cm) or so will be the bottom of the carrier.

❹ Pin the handles, right side out, to the wrong sides of the carrier ends, with an overlap of approximately ¾ inch (2 cm). Stitch them in place with a zigzag stitch to enclose the raw edges as before, then stitch an X pattern for security.

❺ To make the casing for the dowel, fold the carrier in half with the ends together and slip the dowel under the folds of the handles. Mark the stitching line, then stitch across each handle through both thicknesses, backstitching at the ends.

Angel Pillow

DESIGNED BY ANNE McCLOSKEY

Every child can use a guardian angel! This one is worked in shimmery satin and lamé fabrics for a celestial effect. For a more down-to-earth angel, try the same design with scraps of printed and textured cotton. The finished size is 18 inches (45.5 cm) square.

Materials

- Purple satin for pillow front, 19 inches (48.5 cm) square

- Purple cotton for pillow back, the same size (see Options)

- Low-loft fusible batting for pillow front

- Scraps for the angel dress, features, hair, and wings

- Scraps for moon and stars

- Paper-backed fusible web

- Purchased ribbon roses: 3 red and 2 gold

- Purchased tassel trim

- Rayon thread for satin stitch in colors to match appliqué pieces

- Embroidery floss for French knots

- Polyester fiberfill or 18-inch (45.5-cm) pillow form

Instructions

1 Enlarge the pattern and cut out the paper pieces.

2 Press the fusible web to the wrong side of fabrics to be used for appliqué, following the manufacturer's instructions. Outline or trace the appliqué shapes, upside down, on the wrong side of the fused fabric.

3 Arrange the appliqué pieces on the pillow front, keeping them at least 1 inch (2.5 cm) from the edges. Mark the positions. Layer the pieces of the angel this way: arms, legs, face, and wings; then the dress; then the hair. Fuse the pieces in place.

4 Fuse batting to the wrong side of the piece.

5 Stitch a contrast belt on the angel's dress, if desired.

6 Work satin stitch around the angel and dress, and around the stars and moon.

7 Using the photo as a guide, machine quilt in a random pattern on the angel's dress and hair, and on the background.

8 Work French knots (page 15) with several strands of embroidery floss for the angel's facial features and in random spots on the dress and background. Sew ribbon roses and tassel trim in place.

9 Fuse batting to the wrong side of the pillow front, following the manufacturer's instructions.

10 Place cover back and front with right sides together and stitch around the edges with ½ inch (1.5 cm) seam allowance, leaving an opening on one side for turning and stuffing. If a pillow form will be used, leave most of one side open. Trim corners, turn, and press. Stuff, or insert the pillow form, then stitch across the opening.

Options

With the addition of a back zipper, the cover can be removed for laundering or dry cleaning. Cut two pieces for the back, 19 by 10 inches (48.5 by 25.75 cm). Machine baste the two with right sides together along a 19-inch (48.5-cm) side. Press the seam open and install a centered zipper. Stitch securely across the zipper ends. Then construct the cover according to the directions above. If fiberfill will be used instead of a pillow form, make an inner pillow of muslin to use with the removable cover. Cut muslin the same size as the outer pillow front and back.

Hanky Pankies

DESIGNED BY GAY SYMMES

A woman of any age appreciates a gift of pretty lingerie. These panties for little girls feature a yoke or pocket cut from an embroidered or lace-edged handkerchief, giving them an heirloom look without the tedious handwork.

Materials

- Fabric, ⅜ yd (.35 m) lightweight cotton or cotton blend

- Handkerchief

- 1½ yds (1.4 m) elastic, ¼ inch (.7 cm) wide

- 1 yd (1 m) lace, to trim legs (optional)

Panties with pocket

1 Enlarge the pattern and cut out the desired size (panties are sized for girls approximately 2 to 6 years old). Cut front and back from doubled fabric.

2 Cut the pocket pattern that best suits your handkerchief, positioning a decorative corner as shown. For the rectangular pocket, fold under ½ inch (1 cm) along the cut edges, press, and edgestitch to one front section of panties. For the round pocket, machine baste ⅜ inch (1 cm) from the edge around the curve. Gather up the edge, fold along the stitching line, and press to the wrong side. Edgestitch or stitch by hand to one front section.

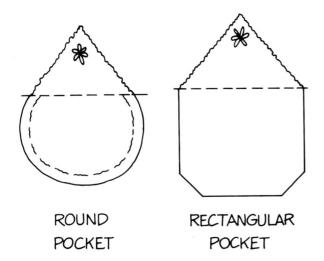

ROUND POCKET

RECTANGULAR POCKET

Note: If the handkerchief has a right and wrong side, apply the pocket wrong side up so the decorative corner will fold to the right side.

3 Sew center front, center back, side seams, and crotch with French seams. To sew a French seam, first stitch the pieces with wrong sides together using ¼ inch (.7 cm) seam allowance. Trim away half the seam allowance and press to one side. Fold along the stitching line with right sides together and stitch again with ¼ inch seam allowance, encasing the raw edges.

4 At the waist, fold ⅝ inch (1.5 cm) to the wrong side and press. Fold under the raw edge ¼ inch (.5 cm), press, and stitch close to the inner fold, leaving an opening to insert the elastic.

5 Cut elastic 1 inch (2.5 cm) smaller than the child's waist measurement. If you aren't sure of the waist size, cut elastic according to pattern size: size 2, 19 inches (48 cm); size 4, 20 inches (51 cm); size 6, 22 inches (56 cm).

6 Insert elastic into the casing and stitch the ends together securely. Close the opening.

7 Measure leg elastic as for waist, cut to size: size 2, 11 inches (28 inches); size 4, 12 inches(30.5 cm); size 6, 13 inches (33 cm).

8 Form casings and insert elastic around the legs as for the waist. If you use lace trim, attach it after pressing the casing but before inserting the elastic. Sew it to the very edge of the leg with a narrow zigzag stitch.

Panties with yoke

1 Cut a corner from the handkerchief so that you have a piece not more than approximately 4 inches (10 cm) wide at the diagonal cut edge, and adding ¾ inch (2 cm) at that edge for seam allowance.

2 Make the panties according to the instructions above through step 3. Press the waistline casing as described in step 4, then open up the outer fold and place the handkerchief right side against the wrong side of the panties front, aligning the diagonal cut edge with the outer fold of the casing. Stitch along the inner fold of the casing, incorporating the handkerchief.

3 Insert the elastic in the casing, close the opening, and fold the handkerchief to the right side. Tack it in place at the front seam. Continue with the instructions above.

Hanky Pankies

Seam allowance included
Patterns are 50% of actual size

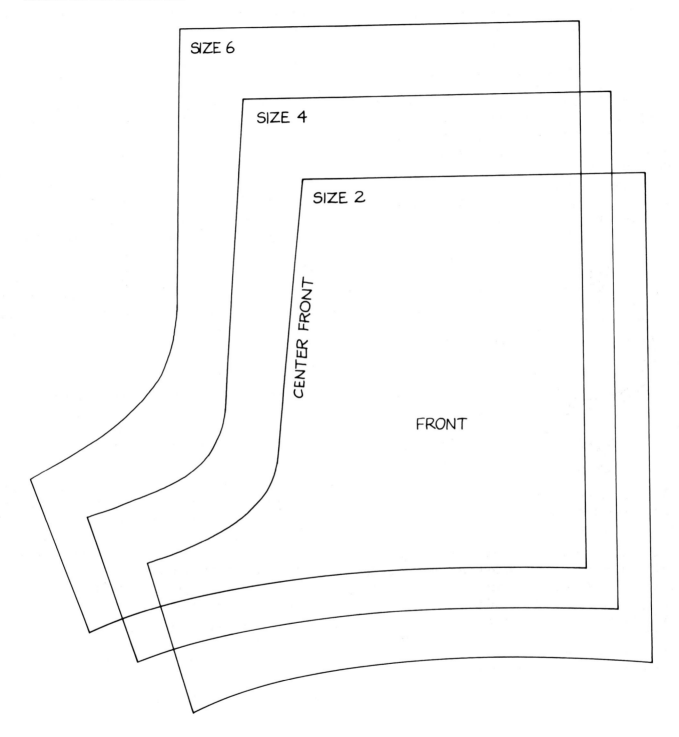

SIZE 6

SIZE 4

SIZE 2

CENTER FRONT

FRONT

Hanky Pankies

Seam allowance included
Patterns are 50% of actual size

SIZE 6

SIZE 4

SIZE 2

CENTER BACK

BACK

Refrigerator Magnets

In homes where the refrigerator serves as Information Central, there are never quite enough magnets to anchor all the important papers. You can create an array of ornamental magnets in an hour with a handful of tiny fabric scraps and sew-on magnets from a craft store.

Make use of motifs cut from printed fabrics as in the photo, or personalize one for each member of the household. You'll think of dozens of ways to decorate your magnets too, with colorful embroidery, painted designs, or simple beadwork.

Materials

- Fabric scraps
- Low-loft batting
- Sew-on magnet
- Washable or disappearing fabric marker (for the personalized magnet)

Instructions

Motif magnets

❶ Cut a motif from printed fabric, allowing ½ inch (1.5 cm) or so around the edges. Cut a scrap of solid-colored fabric the same size for the back. Cut three pieces of batting this size.

❷ Sandwich the fabrics, right sides out, with the batting between.

❸ Outline the motif with a fairly short straight stitch. (An appliqué presser foot makes it easier to see where you're going and to sew around curves). Stitch along some of the design lines to add dimension. Carefully trim close to the outline stitching.

❹ Sew a magnet onto the back.

Personalized magnet

❶ Write the name on a scrap of fabric in fat, bold letters, overlapping them slightly. If you don't feel that artistic, cut the letters you need from a magazine and enlarge them on a photocopier. Cut out and arrange the letters. Tape them together, overlapping them slightly. Trace the outline onto the fabric and mark the intermediate lines for stitching.

❷ Sandwich this piece and a piece for the back, right side out, with three layers of batting between. Stitch around the letters, then trim close to the outer stitching.

❸ Sew the magnet onto the back.

The gift of a handmade garment is twice as impressive when it is accompanied by its own padded hanger. Make a few to brighten your own closet too—they are wonderful for preventing shoulder creases in jackets and blouses. Choose colorfast fabric that won't run or crock onto the garment.

Materials

- Flat wooden hanger

- Fabric

- Lining scraps if necessary (see step 4)

- Polyester fleece, approximately 6 yds (5.5 m) of 1½-inch (4-cm) strips

- Glue stick

- Ribbon, ¾ yd (.7 m)

Instructions

1 Cut two pieces of fabric 3 by 13 inches (7.5 by 33 cm) for the cover top. Cut two pieces 3 by 9 inches (7.5 by 23 cm) for the lower section. Use a mug or other object as a template to cut one rounded end on each piece.

2 Allow ¼ inch (.5 cm) for seams. Gather each top section along the long edges and around the curved end, and sew it to a lower section with right sides together. Turn.

3 Double one end of a fleece strip and fold it over an end of the hanger. Glue or hold it firmly in place and begin at that end to wrap the batting strip around the hanger, keeping the batting taut and overlapping by about ½ inch (1.5 cm). Cut a shorter strip and double it over the other end of the hanger before you wrap to that point. Continue wrapping the hanger until its circumference measures approximately 4½ inches (11.5 cm).

4 If the cover fabric is "sticky"—soft cotton, wool, or the like—wrap the padded hanger with strips of lining fabric so the cover will slip on easily.

5 Pull a cover section over each end of the hanger. At the center, fold under the unfinished end of one section and slip it over the other. Stitch by hand.

6 Fold the ribbon in half and loop it over the neck of the hanger. Bring the ends around the hanger and up through the loop. Pull them tight. Bring one to either side of the neck and tie a bow.

Fabric Gift Bags

DESIGNED BY HARRIET JONES

A gift presented in its own custom-made fabric bag seems more festive. Best of all, the wrapping can be used over and over again. The smallest scrap makes a perfect bag for a gift of jewelry or potpourri. A larger remnant carries a bottle of wine to the dinner party in grand style.

There's no limit to the potential for decoration. These small pieces are wonderful canvases upon which to experiment with your machine's embroidery stitches and to try out the latest decorative threads and fabric paints. To tie the tops of the bags, dig into your collection of short pieces of ribbons and laces.

Materials

- Fabric for outer bag

- Fabric for lining, if desired

- Cord or ribbon

Instructions

Unlined bag

❶ Determine the desired finished size of the bag. Plan for a fold at one side or the bottom if the size of the fabric scrap permits. Add ½ inch (1.5 cm) for seam allowance at the bottom and/or sides. Add 1 inch (2.5 cm) or more for a hem at the top. Cut the piece(s).

❷ Stitch the side and bottom seams. For a bag that is neatly finished inside, make French seams: Stitch with wrong sides together, using half the seam allowance. Trim away half the seam allowance and fold along the seamline with right sides together. Stitch, again using half the seam allowance.

❸ To make a flat bottom on the bag, turn the bag wrong side out and fold it so the bottom seam or fold and one side seam (or fold) are aligned and form a point where they meet. Stitch across the point, perpendicular to the seams. Repeat with the other corner.

❹ Hem the top with a single or double hem, or pink the edges.

Lined bag

❶ Cut outer fabric as described above, but add seam allowance rather than hem allowance at the upper edge. Cut lining the same size.

❷ Stitch the side and bottom seams of the bag and lining, leaving an opening in the bottom or one side of the lining for turning.

❸ With the outer bag wrong side out and the lining right side out, place the lining in the bag and stitch the two together around the upper edge. To form a flat bottom on the bag, see step 3 above. Turn the bag right side out through the lining opening, then stitch the opening.

Fashionable Fabric Doll

DESIGNED BY ANN McCLOSKEY

A new doll will always delight its young recipient. Make this one of plain muslin to outfit in style, or make it of soft, lightweight fabric—perhaps a floral print cotton flannel—just to hug. Our doll sports a festive sundress that's quick to assemble from scraps of wire-edged fabric ribbon. If time is short, make the dress for a 12-inch (30-cm) purchased muslin doll.

Materials

For the doll:

- Fabric, approximately ¼ yd (.25 m)
- Loose fiberfill for stuffing
- Acrylic paints or fabric markers for facial features, if desired

For the dress:

- 1 yd (1 m) wire-edged cotton ribbon, 6 inches (15 cm) wide
- 2½ yds (1.4 m) wire-edged ribbon, 3 inches (7.5 cm) wide
- For the choker, a length of ribbon and small button or charm

For a very young child, substitute strips of fabric or fabric ribbon without wire. Hem one edge and machine gather the other, then follow the instructions below.

Instructions

Doll

Sew all seams with right sides together and ¼ inch (.7 cm) seam allowance.

1. Trace the pattern and cut the pieces from double thickness fabric. Transfer markings.

Tip: For a larger or smaller doll, enlarge or reduce the pattern on a photocopier. Remember, the seam allowances will be altered too.

2. Stitch the leg sections together. Leave open across the tops and between notches. Clip curves and turn right side out. Baste to body front with right sides together.

3. Stitch body center back seam, leaving open between notches.

4. Stitch body front to body back with right sides together, tucking the legs inside. Clip curves and turn.

5. Stuff the form with fiberfill and hand stitch across the openings.

6. To define shoulders, elbows, and knees, stitch as indicated by the dotted lines on the pattern.

Doll Dress

1. Wrap a length of 3-inch (7.5-cm) ribbon around shoulders for straps, then around the chest for the dress top. Trim at center back and stitch ends together.

2. For the skirt, gather the 6-inch (15-cm) ribbon by pulling the wire along one side of the ribbon. Overlap the edges in back, tie the wires, and stitch the fabric edges.

3. For each sleeve, gather a circle of the narrower ribbon to fit around the shoulder. Sew the ends together, and stitch to the shoulder strap.

4. With narrower ribbon, form a turban around the head and stitch on a decorative bow.

5. Cut a length of narrow ribbon for the choker and sew it at the back of the neck. Sew on the charm or button.

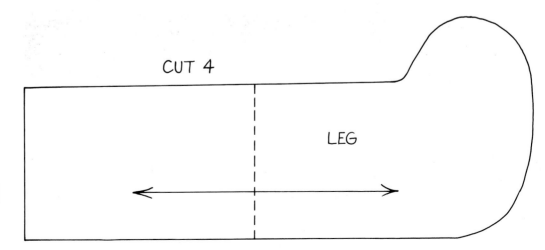

CUT 4

LEG

Fashionable Fabric Doll

Seam allowance included
Pattern is 50% of actual size

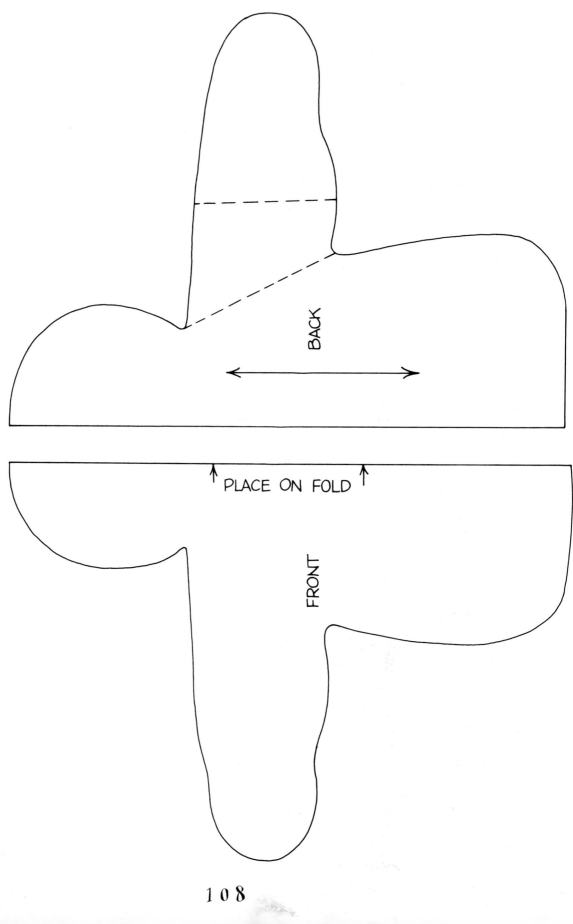

Fashionable
Fabric Doll

*Seam allowance
included*

*Pattern is 50% of
actual size*

BACK

PLACE ON FOLD

FRONT

Fabric scraps and remnants can be assembled into a variety of useful accessories for the office, home, and points between. We've provided the basic instructions; it's up to you to add the imaginative embellishments.

Outfitting the Office

Bless computers for the time and effort they save us but, let's admit it, they are not particularly attractive. Custom covers will hide their beigeness when they're not in service and will keep the components free of dust besides.

For these covers we have used scraps from a reupholstering project and ornamented them with stripes of bright grosgrain ribbon and a few buttons and beads. Cotton fabric is a good choice because it is relatively free of static. Since components vary greatly in size, fabric requirements for these pieces are not given. The instructions for each cover tell how to figure the yardage you will need.

A note of caution: The computer processor requires ventilation. Remove the cover when you use the computer, then let it cool to the touch after you turn it off before replacing the cover.

DESIGNED BY JOYCE BALDWIN

Keyboard Cover

If you will add machine-sewn decorations, it is easiest to sew them in place before constructing the cover.

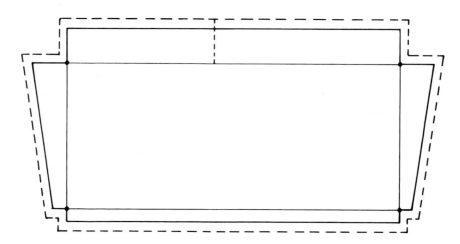

For the keyboard cover pattern, first measure the keyboard width and length and draw a rectangle.

1 Make a paper pattern. Measure the width and depth of the keyboard and add approximately ¼ inch (.5 cm) to each measurement for ease. Draw a rectangle this size to represent the top of the keyboard. Mark each corner with a dot.

2 Measure height, front and back. On the diagram, extend the back and front by these measurements.

3 For the sides, extend at the back by the back height measurement and at the front by the front height measurement. Draw a line on each side to connect the two points.

4 Add hem allowance at all edges and seam allowance at the corners. Your pattern should resemble the diagram. Allow for the cord connection. Ours is at center back and placement is marked with a dotted line.

5 Cut fabric to the pattern. Transfer the corner dots.

6 Add ornamentation to the cover according to your plan. Keep in mind the hem and seam allowances.

7 Fold and stitch the corner seams from edges to the marked dots. Press them open and clean-finish the seam allowances.

8 Slash the fabric as necessary to accommodate the cord. Fold the edges to the wrong side, clean-finish them, and edgestitch along both folds.

9 Hem the cover.

Processor Cover

If your monitor sits on top of the processor, you may want to make a cover that serves both pieces. Look at the instructions for the monitor cover that follow.

Instructions

1 Draw a diagram with the processor measurements. Measure the width and depth of the top. Note the locations of cord connections. Add approximately ¼ inch (.5 cm) ease to each measurement for medium-weight fabric, slightly more for very heavy fabric. Add seam and hem allowances.

2 Cut the fabric to these measurements. Mark seamline intersections at the corners.

3 Construct the cover according to the instructions for the keyboard cover, steps 5 through 9.

Monitor Cover

Because of its irregular lines, the easiest way to plan this cover is to drape a piece of fabric over your monitor, then pin and mark the seam and hemlines. If you will be working with a single large piece of fabric, you can use the actual cover fabric for this step. Position it wrong side out for marking. If you are the cautious type, use a large piece of muslin and make a pattern first. To cover a monitor and processor together, as shown in the photo, just lengthen it accordingly.

Instructions

1 Arrange the fabric over the monitor so that the lengthwise grain runs straight down the front and back of the monitor and the crossgrain is straight down the sides. It may be helpful to define the grainlines with a marker.

2 Pinch up the corners and pin to fit. Allow a little ease so the cover won't be too tight. Mark the edges of the monitor top. Mark the hemlines and cord locations.

3 Remove the cover and draw along both sides of each pinned seam with a fabric marker. Remove the pins. Match up the two front corners and the two back corners. Neaten the seam and hemlines. Add seam and hem allowances.

4 Use the muslin to cut the cover fabric. You may want to baste the corner seams and check the fit before stitching permanently.

5 Stitch the corner seams. If necessary to accommodate the cord connection, slash from the lower edge to the marked point and hem the cut edges. Hem the cover.

Tip: If there is a chance you might upgrade your equipment before you next redecorate, use wide seam and hem allowances and sew the cover with the longest stitch length that will hold. You will be able to alter the cover to fit the new components.

Mouse House

(shown in the photo on page 110, lower right)

First plan the ornamentation you will add. For machine-sewn embellishments, it is easiest to add them before the seams are sewn. Remember to allow for the seam and hem allowances.

Instructions

1 To determine fabric width, measure the circumference of the mouse at the widest point. Divide by two, and add 1½ inches (4 cm) for seam allowances and ease. For length, measure the circumference of the mouse at the longest point and add 2½ inches (6 cm) for hem allowance. Cut fabric this size.

2 Fold the piece in half across the width with right sides together and stitch the side seams. Overcast the seam allowances if the fabric tends to ravel.

3 Fold the upper edge 1¼ inches (3 cm) to the wrong side; press. Fold under the raw edge ¼ inch (.5 cm); press. For very heavy fabric, overcast this edge instead. Stitch the hem.

DESIGNED BY JOYCE BALDWIN

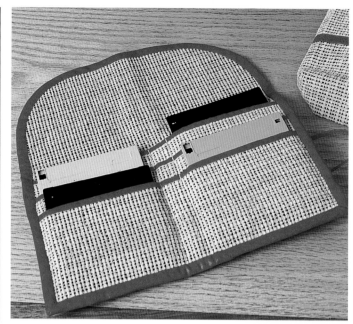

DESIGNED BY JOYCE BALDWIN

Disk Carriers

When your work travels with you, protect your valuable disks in a convenient—and pretty—fabric case. The smaller carrier holds six 3½-inch (9-cm) disks, the larger one accommodates six CDs or 5 ¼-inch (13.5-cm) disks.

Materials

- The outer part of the case is best made with heavy fabric, such as denim, upholstery fabric, or pre-quilted material. Use a lightweight fabric for lining. If you choose two thinner fabrics, add a layer of garment-weight batting in between.

- Fabric for outer case and pockets

- Fabric for lining

- Batting, if needed

- Double-fold bias binding ⅜ inch (1 cm) wide, 2¾ yds (2.55 m) for the larger case or 2¼ yds (2.1 m) for the smaller. To make your own binding, see page 52.

- Button

Instructions

❶ Cut outer fabric, lining, and batting for the small case 10 inches (25 cm) wide and 10½ inches (26.5 cm) long. For the large case cut these pieces 13 inches (33 cm) wide and 12 inches (30.5 cm) long. Using a cup or template, round the two top corners of these pieces. Cut three pockets the width of the case and 3¼ inches (8 cm) long for the small case; 4½ inches (11.5 cm) long for the large case. Mark the lengthwise center of all pieces.

❷ If batting is used, baste to wrong side of outer piece. Sew a button on the right side, approximately 1 inch (2.5 cm) from the right edge and 3 inches (8 cm) above the lower edge.

❸ For the button loop, cut a strip of bias binding 6½ inches (16.5 cm) long and stitch the folded long edges together. Place it at the corresponding position at the left end of the carrier on the outer side, loop ends aligned with the carrier edge. Baste.

❹ Apply bias binding to the upper long edge of each pocket (instructions are on page 53). Overcast the lower long edges.

❺ Place the upper pocket, right side up, on the lining right side, the pocket lower edge 2 inches (5 cm) above the lining lower edge. Stitch along the lower edge of the pocket with a zigzag stitch.

❻ Position and stitch the center pocket at its placement line in the same way. Place the lower pocket along the lower edge of the lining and stitch once, close to the edge.

❼ Place the outer case and lining with wrong sides together (the batting between) and baste together around the outer edge, stitching close to the edge.

❽ Work two lines of stitching ⅜ inch (.7 cm) apart at the center of the carrier from the lower edge to the top, creating six pockets.

❾ Apply bias binding around the outer edge.

Options

Add a business card holder to identify the carrier as your own. Cut a piece of 40-gauge clear vinyl ⅜ inch (1 cm) larger all around than the card. Before the pockets are sewn to the carrier, center the vinyl piece on one side of the lower pocket section. Sew around the sides and lower edge with a zigzag stitch.

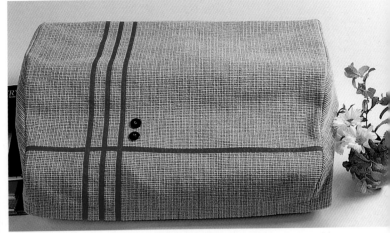

DESIGNED BY JOYCE BALDWIN

Typewriter Cover

Some of us will never give up our typewriters! And most of them have outlasted their factory-issue vinyl covers. It takes just a short time to make the handsome new one that your typewriter has surely earned.

Instructions

❶ Make a paper pattern. For the central section, measure from the table, over the machine from front to back. Measure the width of the body of the machine (at more than one point if necessary), and add ease equal to about half the combined width of the carriage return knobs.

For the sides, hold a piece of paper flat against the machine and mark around the edges with a fingernail. The piece should extend to the table at the lower edge. The length of this piece along the curved edge should equal the length of the central piece.

Add generous seam and hem allowances to both pieces.

❷ Cut one central section, and cut the sides from doubled fabric.

❸ Baste the seams, check the fit, then stitch permanently. Add decorations. Stitch the hems.

Options

If your typewriter is a vintage model with a long-handled carriage return, leave an opening for it at the appropriate place in a seam or work a large buttonhole with a scrap of interfacing on the wrong side of the cover to reinforce behind it.

Teapot Parka

DESIGNED BY FLETA MONAGHAN

Materials

- Paper, to make a pattern

- Outer fabric, enough for main pattern pieces, four shoulder strap pieces, and small pieces for trim

- Lining, the same quantity as outer fabric

- Thick fusible batting, the same quantity as lining

- Small scraps of complementary fabric for pockets and front band

- Strip of complementary fabric for belt

- Synthetic fur scraps approximately 1 inch (2.5 cm) in width, one piece the circumference of the cover's lower edge and one piece for the "collar"

- Small belt buckle

- Decorative button

I t's not the traditional tea cozy, but it will keep the tea pot hot and the contents steaming. A matching coaster insulates the bottom of the pot against a cold kitchen counter.

We chose green taffeta for the outer cover and rosy pink for the lining, with synthetic fur for trim. Look through your scrap and button collections for inspiration as to accents, and make your cover unique!

Instructions

Make a pattern. Measure one end of the pot to the other at widest point, from center of spout to center of handle. For height, measure center of lid to surface upon which the pot is sitting. Add approximately 1 inch (2.5 cm) ease to your measurements, and make a paper pattern. If your tea pot is a standard shape, the pattern should resemble the illustration. Tape the pattern pieces together to try it on the pot for fit; it should be a bit roomy, as the thickness of the fabrics will take up some of the ease.

Cutting Out

1 Cut batting from this pattern version, then add seam allowance and cut outer fabric and lining.

2 Make the coaster pattern. For the coaster, measure the width of the parka pattern at the lower edge. Double this measurement to get the circumference of the coaster pattern. Use a flexible tape measure to shape a rough oval on the paper, then fold the paper in quarters to even up the curves.

3 Cut batting from this pattern, then add seam allowances to cut outer fabrics.

4 Cut two pockets and one front band piece, adding a narrow hem/seam allowance at all edges. The front band extends from the cover lower edge to approximately 1 inch (2.5 cm) below the upper seam.

5 Cut the shoulder strap/belt carrier pieces. Determine the finished width (ours are 1¼ inches or 3.2 cm). Cut two pieces, twice this width plus ½ inch (1.4 cm) for ¼-inch (.7-cm) seam allowances. In length, figure the distance from the upper seam to the top of the pocket, and add approximately 2 inches (6 cm).

6 For the belt, cut a strip twice as wide as the desired finished width, plus seam allowances. In length, cut it approximately three times the width of the cover pattern piece.

Assembly

1 With right sides together, stitch long edges and one end of each shoulder strap piece. Turn; press.

2 Fold belt piece in half lengthwise, wrong side out. Stitch long edge and ends, angling each end to a point at one side, and leaving an opening on the long edge for turning. Turn, press, and stitch the opening.

3 Press under the seam allowances on the long edges and upper end of the band. Position it at the center of the cover front, lower raw edges aligned. Topstitch it in place.

4 Press under the seam allowances on the pockets. Stitch across the upper edge of each. Position on the cover front and topstitch in place along the sides and across the lower edge.

5 Fold shoulder strap pieces in half lengthwise, wrong side out. Stitch long edge and straight across one end of each. Turn right side out; press. Pin to the cover front, unfinished ends aligned with the cover upper edge and finished ends tucked into the pockets. Baste upper ends to the cover seam allowance.

6 Fuse batting to the wrong side of the cover front and back sections, inside the seamlines, following manufacturer's instructions. Fuse batting to one coaster section.

7 Stitch cover front to back, right sides together, along sides and across top. Stitch lining pieces the same way. Press. Stitch cover to lining around the lower edges with right sides together, leaving approximately 4 inches (10 cm) open for turning. Turn and press. Press under the seam allowances at the opening (the opening will be stitched closed when the trim is applied).

8 Stitch fur trim around the lower edge and at the "neckline."

9 Arrange the belt through the shoulder strap carriers and fasten it with the buckle. Sew on the neckline button.

10 Stitch coaster to its lining with right sides together, leaving an opening for turning. Clip the seam allowance at intervals, cutting almost to the stitching line. Turn, press, and stitch the opening.

Jewelry Protectors

DESIGNED BY
JUDITH ROBERTSON

Honor a cherished piece of jewelry with its own custom-sized silk case, lined with silvercloth to ward off tarnish. These cases make good travelers, too, protecting jewelry pieces from bumps and scrapes and preventing tangles.

We've chosen two styles that accommodate most jewelry shapes. The long case is just right for a bracelet or necklace and the drawstring pouch holds earrings, a pin, or a watch.

Silvercloth is available from well-stocked fabric stores and mail order sources. It should not be preshrunk before sewing. Laundering or dry cleaning will remove the anti-tarnish properties.

Materials

- Silk or other fabric for outer case

- Silvercloth

- Thick, rather firm interfacing

- Large snap, for the long case

- Rattail cord or ribbon, for the drawstring pouch

Long case

1 Determine the finished size of the case, adding a little ease to the actual measurements of the piece. Allow ¼ inch (.7 cm) for all seams.

2 Cut outer fabric four times the length (height) of the case plus ½ inch (1.5 cm) seam allowance, and cut to the finished width plus ½ inch (1.5 cm) seam allowance. Cut interfacing the same width, but in length three times the finished length measurement plus seam allowances. Cut silvercloth the same width, and in length cut it twice the finished length measurement plus seam allowances.

3 Position interfacing on the wrong side of the outer fabric, aligning the lower edges and sides. Baste just outside the seamlines and trim away the excess. (We chose sew-in interfacing for this light-weight silk fabric, but fusible would work well with other fabrics. For fusible, trim away the seam allowances before bonding to the fabric.)

4 With right sides together, sew silvercloth to fabric along the upper and lower edges. Press.

5 Fold the piece so that one fabric/lining seam is at the bottom and the upper edge of the interfacing at the top. Stitch the sides, leaving an opening at about the center of one side for turning. Trim, and turn right side out.

6 With the piece lining side up, fold the lower third upward. Stitch together at the sides by hand or with a machine edgestitch.

7 Fold the flap down and mark positions for one or two snaps.

8 A silk-covered snap makes an elegant closure. Here's how to make them: For each snap, cut two circles of lightweight silk approximately twice the diameter of the snap. Overcast around the edge of each circle by hand. Without breaking the thread, put a snap section face down on the center of the circle and draw up the circle around it. On the ball section, pierce a tiny hole in the silk over the center of the ball and force the ball through it. Take several stitches across the back to tighten the silk and secure the edges. Sew at the marked position.

Drawstring pouch

1 Determine the finished size of the case, adding a little ease to the actual measurements of the piece and allowing for the drawstring casing at the top of the bag. Allow ¼ inch (.7 cm) for all seams.

2 For the outer fabric, to the finished measurements add ¾ inch (2 cm) at the upper edge and seam allowances on all four sides. Cut two. For the silvercloth lining, cut two pieces the same width as the outer fabric but 1½ inches (4 cm) shorter in length. Cut sew-in interfacing the same size as the lining. Cut fusibles this size less the seam allowances.

3 Fuse or baste to the lining sections and trim away excess seam allowance. For sew-in, trim away seam allowances.

4 With right sides together, sew the lining sections together at the sides and lower edge, leaving an opening at the bottom for turning.

5 Pin the outer fabric pieces with right sides together. On one side seam, sew from the upper edge for ¼ inch (.7 cm). Then leave 1½ (4 cm) inches open. Stitch the remainder of the side and across the bottom. Stitch the other side, leaving an opening as on the first side. Trim the corners, and press under the seam allowances along the openings.

6 With the outer bag wrong side out and the lining right side out, place the lining in the bag and stitch the two together around the upper edge. Turn the bag right side out through the lining opening, then stitch the opening.

7 Cut two pieces of rattail cord or ribbon, each approximately four times the width of the bag. Thread one piece through both sides of the casing at the bag's upper edge and knot the ends together. Start the second cord on the opposite side of the bag and thread it through in the same way.

Woven Loop Potholders

Remember these? Woven potholders recall drizzly afternoons at summer camp when you would rather have been swimming. From a utilitarian point of view, there isn't a potholder that works better. And they still provide rainy-day fun for kids of any age. After a long absence, potholder looms are once again available from mail order sources and at craft stores. Easiest to use is a model with metal prongs that bend slightly outward to keep the loops securely in place.

All-cotton knit fabrics, or polyester-cotton blends make the best loops. Avoid acrylics; contact with a hot oven rack can melt them.

Materials

- Scraps of cotton knit fabrics and/or old T-shirts
- Potholder loom

Helpful, but not essential:

- Rotary cutter and mat

Instructions

Knits vary greatly in their stretchability. In any one potholder, it is best to combine fabrics with the same amount of stretch so the potholder won't have wavy edges. Test the stretchability of the fabrics you plan to use.

1. Cut a one-inch (2.5-cm) crossgrain strip of each fabric and determine the length to cut the strips. Stretch the sample strip across the loom. It should be taut enough to stay in place without sagging, but not guitar-string tight.

2. Cut the scraps into rectangles, the crossgrain width determined by the measurement from step 1 with approximately ⅜ inch (1 cm) seam allowance added, and whatever length you are able to get from the piece.

3. Fold each square in half lengthwise, wrong side out, and stitch the ends to form a tube. Use a secure overcast stitch designed for knits, if possible, or a medium-width zigzag stitch set for a fairly short stitch length.

4. Cut each tube into loops. Make them approximately 1 inch (2.5 cm) wide if the knit is thin, to approximately ¾ inch (2 cm) for heavier fabric.

5. In case it never rained at your camp, here's how to make the potholder: Stretch a loop across the loom between each pair of pegs. Weave the hook through the loops, over both strands of a loop then under both strands of the next. Put the end of a new loop on the hook, and draw it through, securing it on the first empty pair of pegs. Repeat with another loop and the next pair of empty pegs, alternating the over-under pattern. Tighten each loop against the preceding one so they are straight.

6. When the weaving is complete, finish the edges. Starting at the right end of the side of the loom away from you, slip the small end of the hook from right to left through two loops. Slip the first loop on the hook over the second. Slip the hook through the next loop on the loom, slip the loop already on the hook over it and off, and so on. When one loop remains on the hook, pull it up sharply to use as a hanging loop.

Lingerie Laundry Bags

uarantee your delicate laundry a safe trip through the washer in its own lacy bag. A remnant of synthetic tablecloth or curtain lace with one decoratively finished edge calls a halt to knotted straps and lost stockings. If you don't have such a remnant, perhaps you finally have a reason to replace those lace curtains you've looked at long enough, but which refuse to wear out.

The bags illustrated are approximately 12 inches (30.5 cm) square. Each has a double layer of lace, the bag itself underneath and an "overskirt" that makes use of the fabric's decorative edge.

DESIGNED BY MARY PARKER

Materials

- Synthetic lace fabric remnants (see step 1)

- Snap tape, 12 inches (30.5 cm)

Instructions

1 For the under bag, cut a piece of lace, without a finished edge, 13 by 25 inches (33 by 63 cm). Cut a second piece 12½ by 25 inches (32 by 63 cm), one long side on the finished edge of the lace.

2 For the under bag, fold the lace piece in half across its length, right sides together. Stitch the sides (adjacent to the fold), then trim and overcast the seam allowances. As an alternative, use a serger rolled hem stitch to sew the seams.

3 Fold the other lace piece the same way, and stitch together the edges *opposite* the fold, forming a tube with the finished edge of the lace at one end.

4 With both pieces right side out, place the bag into the tube, aligning their unfinished edges. Turn these edges together ½ inch (1.5 cm) to the inside of the bag and baste.

5 Sew snap tape to the inside of the bag on both sides, turning under the ends and placing the tape edges just below the folded edge of the bag. Take care that the snap halves are opposite one another.

Options

Mary Jane Parks, who has spent a good part of her life sorting socks for four daughters and five grandchildren, offers this suggestion: Make a bag for each child in the house. Add a name tag or monogram (use a scrap of sturdier fabric, then zigzag it to the bag) and a loop for hanging. Keep the bag on the child's closet doorknob to collect dirty socks. On laundry day, bag and contents go through the washer and dryer then back to their rightful owner with no sorting needed.

Hanger Coats

DESIGNED BY JOYCE BALDWIN

Colorful padded hanger covers do wonders for a dreary closet. Better still, they help keep clothes neat and ready to wear. This one is designed to fit a standard plastic hanger that has been padded with batting.

To edge the covers, use purchased bias tape or make your own with a bias tape maker and strips of the cover fabric. (See pages 52 and 53 for details.) Add a monogram if you wish, or use a plain fabric and quilt it to the batting with an embroidery stitch and decorative thread.

Materials

- Plastic hanger, standard size

- Fabric scrap to fit the pattern, or piece small scraps to size (instructions are on page 000)

- Fusible batting

- Thick batting, approximately 24 by 14 inches (61 by 36 cm)

- Double-fold bias tape, approximately 2½ yds (2.3 m), ¼ inch (.7 cm) wide

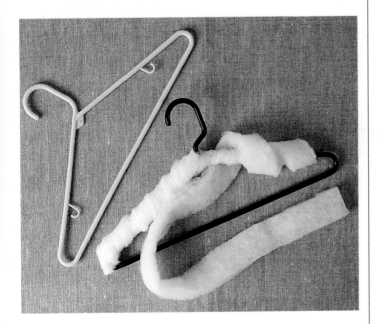

Instructions

Preshrink all fabrics to make a hanger cover that will be washable.

1 Enlarge the pattern and cut it from paper. Use the pattern as a guide for cutting outer fabric, lining, and batting, allowing an extra ½ inch (1.5 cm) or so around all edges.

2 Fuse batting to the wrong side of the lining fabric. Pin-baste this piece to the outer cover wrong side.

3 Machine quilt through all layers in the pattern of your choice. Mark the pattern outline on the piece. Baste around the edges, just outside the marked line. Trim close to the stitching.

4 Apply bias binding to the center front edges, following the instructions on page 53.

5 Cut a length of tape long enough to bind the neck edge and extend approximately 9 inches (23 cm) on each side for the ties. Sew it in place and continue stitching along the tie ends.

6 With right sides together, stitch the ends of the cover as indicated on the pattern. Press the seam open and overcast the seam allowances.

7 Apply bias binding around the lower edge, again extending the binding at center front for ties. Knot the tie ends.

8 Cut the fleece into strips approximately 1½ inches (4 cm) wide. Wrap around the upper part of the hanger to pad it, as shown in the photograph. Stitch the end of the fleece in place. Cover the hanger and tie bows at the front.

Hanger Coats

Add seam allowance according to instructions
Pattern is 50% of actual size

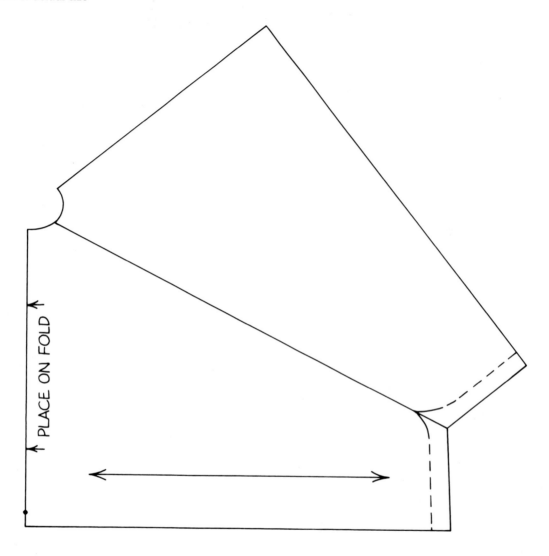

PLACE ON FOLD

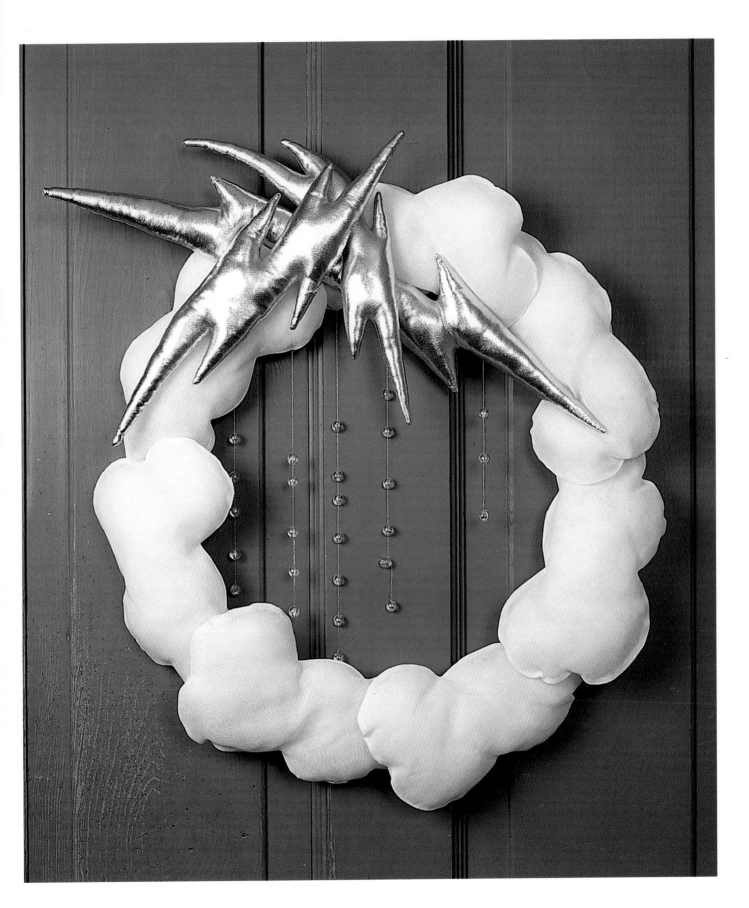

The Designers

We wish to thank all the talented designers who engineered and executed the projects shown on the preceding pages. They have shared not only their ideas and patterns, but many valuable sewing tips gleaned from their own experience.

Judy Anderson
Goodlettsville, Tennessee
pages 12, 13

Joyce Baldwin
Cullowhee, North Carolina
pages 62, 110, 112, 113, 120

Becky Brodersen
Nashville, Tennessee
page 18

Chris Bryant
Asheville, North Carolina
page 105

Xanath Espina
Asheville, North Carolina
page 27

Beth Hill
Asheville, North Carolina
page 57

Harriet Jones
Nashville, Tennessee
page 104

Lori Kerr
Durham, North Carolina
pages 9, 71, 83

Susan Kinney
Asheville, North Carolina
page 32

Ann McCloskey
Copley, Ohio
pages 25, 94, 106

Fleta Monaghan
Asheville, North Carolina
pages 39, 114

Mary Parker
Asheville, North Carolina
pages 19, 20, 23, 48, 80, 119

Carol Parks
Asheville, North Carolina
pages 33, 60, 101, 102, 118

Judith Robertson
Asheville, North Carolina
page 116

Bird Ross
Madison, Wisconsin
pages 28, 36, 65

Maggie Rotman
Asheville, North Carolina
page 54

Brenda Sconyers
Asheville, North Carolina
page 38

Pat Scheible
Mebane, North Carolina
page 42

Acknowledgements

Our sincere thanks to the following businesses and their proprietors, who graciously entrusted us with priceless treasures from their shops for our photography sessions:

Liz Spear
Waynesville, North Carolina
pages 74, 76, 77

Gay Symmes
Asheville, North Carolina
pages 84, 97

Pat Taylor
Winston-Salem, North Carolina
pages 11, 81, 86, 90

Terry Taylor
Asheville, North Carolina
pages 45, 78, 92

Dee Dee Triplett
Bryson City, North Carolina
page 34

Sandy Webster
Brasstown, North Carolina
pages 16, 17

Mary Kay West
Asheville, North Carolina
pages 68, 70

Magnolia Beauregard's

Native Expressions

The Natural Home

Preservation Hall Architectural Salvage

Index

Projects

Techniques